LSAT®

PrepTest 80

Unlocked

Exclusive Data, Analysis & Explanations for the December 2016 LSAT

PUBLISHING

New York

© 2017 by Kaplan, Inc.

Published by Kaplan Publishing, a division of Kaplan, Inc.
750 Third Avenue
New York, NY 10017

ISBN: 978-1-5062-2339-1
10 9 8 7 6 5 4 3 2 1

The Inside Story

PrepTest 80 was administered in December 2016. It challenged 31,340 test takers. What made this test so hard? Here's a breakdown of what Kaplan students who were surveyed after taking the official exam considered PrepTest 80's most difficult section.

Hardest PrepTest 80 Section as Reported by Test Takers

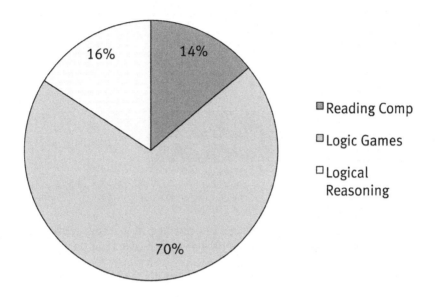

Based on these results, you might think that studying Logic Games is the key to LSAT success. Well, Logic Games is important, but test takers' perceptions don't tell the whole story. For that, you need to consider students' actual performance. The following chart shows the average number of students to miss each question in each of PrepTest 80's different sections.

Percentage Incorrect by PrepTest 80 Section Type

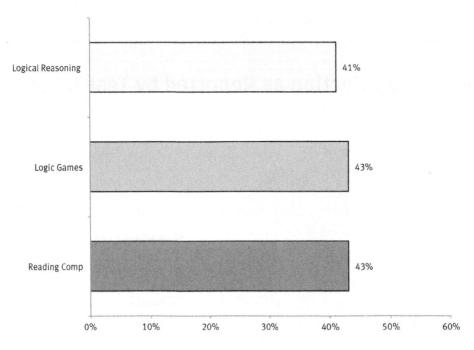

Actual student performance tells quite a different story. On average, students were almost equally likely to miss questions in all three of the different section types, and on PrepTest 80, Reading Comprehension was equal to Logic Games in actual difficulty.

Maybe students overestimate the difficulty of the Logic Games section because it's so unusual, or maybe it's because a really hard Logic Game is so easy to remember after the test. That may have been the case on PrepTest 80, which featured a Process game for the first time in over 20 years! But the truth is that the test maker places hard questions throughout the test. Here were the locations of the 10 hardest (most missed) questions in the exam.

Location of 10 Most Difficult Questions in PrepTest 80

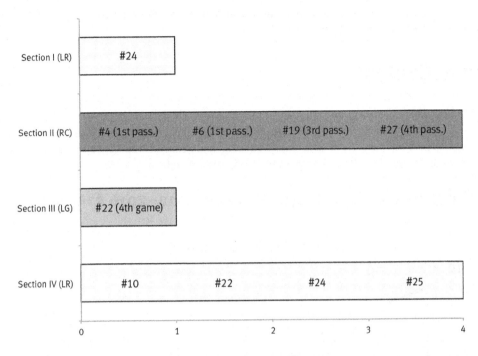

The takeaway from this data is that, to maximize your potential on the LSAT, you need to take a comprehensive approach. Test yourself rigorously, and review your performance on every section of the test. Kaplan's LSAT explanations provide the expertise and insight you need to fully understand your results. The explanations are written and edited by a team of LSAT experts, who have helped thousands of students improve their scores. Kaplan always provides data-driven analysis of the test, ranking the difficulty of every question based on actual student performance. The ten hardest questions on every test are highlighted with a 4-star difficulty rating, the highest we give. The analysis breaks down the remaining questions into 1-, 2-, and 3-star ratings so that you can compare your performance to thousands of other test takers on all LSAC material.

Don't settle for wondering whether a question was really as hard as it seemed to you. Analyze the test with real data, and learn the secrets and strategies that help top scorers master the LSAT.

7 Can't–Miss Features of PrepTest 80

- PrepTest 80 contained the first Process logic game since September 1995 (PT 16). To put how long ago that was in perspective, just a few days after PT 16 was administered OJ Simpson was acquitted of murder.
- Although the star ratings may indicate the fourth game of the section (the Process game) gave some students trouble, that may be simply because they were afraid of the unknown. Check out the explanations to see how easily the game could be handled for those that were willing to do just a little bit of math.
- This was the first PrepTest since June '12 (PT 66) with no Role of a Statement questions. That's a pretty big omission considering there were five Role of a Statement questions on the previous year's December test (PT 77).
- PrepTest 80 featured two Distribution games—which was only the fifth time that had ever happened on a released test. Did you get déjà vu reading that comment? PrepTest 79 *also* had two Distribution games!
- Six Logic Function questions marked the most in a Reading Comprehension section since there were seven in June '04 (PT 43).

- This was not the test to guess (C). Although each answer choice would be expected to show up about 20 percent of the time, (C) was correct less than 14 percent of the time on PrepTest 80, and less than 9 percent of the time in the Logic Games section.
- The second to last question of the test was about rafting across the Pacific Ocean. Coincidentally, the #1 movie at the box office the weekend PrepTest 80 was administered was *Moana*!

PrepTest 80 in Context

As much fun as it is to find out what makes a PrepTest unique or noteworthy, it's even more important to know just how representative it is of other LSAT administrations (and, thus, how likely it is to be representative of the exam you will face on Test Day). The following charts compare the numbers of each kind of question and game on PrepTest 80 to the average numbers seen on all officially released LSATs administered over the past five years (from 2012 through 2016).

Number of LR Questions by Type: PrepTest 80 vs. 2012–2016 Average

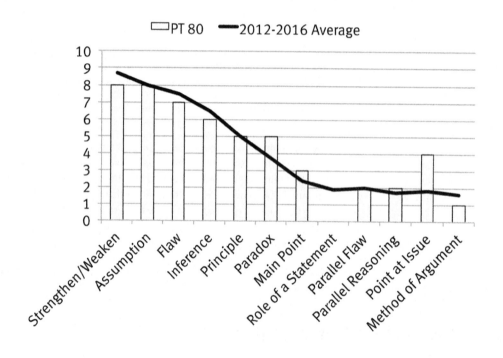

Number of LG Games by Type: PrepTest 80 vs. 2012–2016 Average

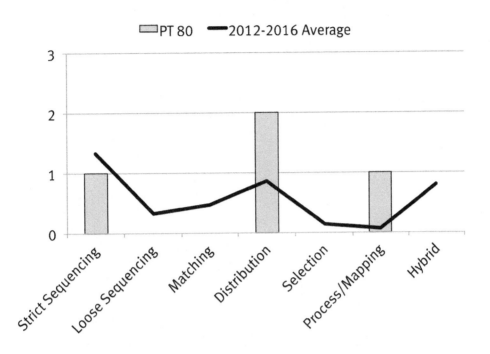

Number of RC Questions by Type: PrepTest 80 vs. 2012–2016 Average

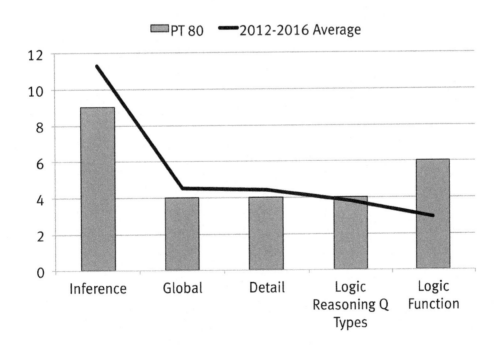

There isn't usually a huge difference in the distribution of questions from LSAT to LSAT, but if this test seems harder (or easier) to you than another you've taken, compare the number of questions of the types on which you, personally, are strongest and weakest. And then explore within each section to see if your best or worst question types came earlier or later.

Students in Kaplan's comprehensive LSAT courses have access to every released LSAT and to an online question bank with thousands of officially released questions, games, and passages. If you are studying on your own, you have to do a bit more work to identify your strengths and your areas of opportunity. Quantitative analysis (like that in the charts above) is an important tool for understanding how the test is constructed and how you are performing on it.

Section I: Logical Reasoning

Q#	Question Type	Correct	Difficulty
1	Paradox	D	★
2	Flaw	A	★★
3	Main Point	A	★
4	Principle (Identify/Strengthen)	E	★
5	Assumption (Necessary)	A	★
6	Main Point	B	★
7	Point at Issue	D	★
8	Paradox	C	★
9	Assumption (Sufficient)	D	★
10	Inference	D	★★
11	Strengthen	D	★
12	Paradox	C	★★
13	Flaw	A	★★
14	Parallel Reasoning	C	★★
15	Point at Issue	C	★
16	Flaw	B	★★★
17	Assumption (Necessary)	E	★★★
18	Point at Issue (Agree)	D	★★★
19	Weaken	A	★★★
20	Method of Argument	A	★★★
21	Principle (Apply/Inference)	B	★★★
22	Inference	D	★★★
23	Strengthen	E	★★★
24	Parallel Flaw	E	★★★★
25	Assumption (Necessary)	C	★★

1. (D) Paradox

Step 1: Identify the Question Type

The question asks for something that will "resolve the apparent conflict." That means there will be a mystery to be solved, making this a Paradox question.

Step 2: Untangle the Stimulus

A study consisted of two groups of dust-mite allergy sufferers. The first group slept on a bed with mite-proof bedding, while the other group slept on a bed without such bedding. Bedding is said to be the primary source of dust mites. Still, the special bedding provided no relief to its users, even though it reduced dust-mite allergens by 69%.

Step 3: Make a Prediction

If bedding is such a major source of dust mites, why are people with dust-mite protection still suffering? The correct answer will solve this mystery. Most likely, those people are suddenly getting exposed to a lot more dust mites elsewhere, or a 69% reduction—no matter how great that sounds—is still just not enough to reduce symptoms.

Step 4: Evaluate the Answer Choices

(D) resolves the issue. If sufferers need a 90–95% reduction to get relief, then a 69% reduction is nice but just not good enough to provide relief.

(A) is a 180. This just confirms that dust-mite allergens in bedding are particularly irritating. That makes it even more unusual that the special bedding didn't help.

(B) is Out of Scope. Exaggerated or not, people's reports were no different with or without the bedding. This doesn't explain why people didn't experience *any* relief, even with the special bedding.

(C) is also Out of Scope. It doesn't matter that the cause of the allergy isn't *fully* understood. It's still caused by dust-mite allergens in some way, and reducing those allergens should have reduced some symptoms—but that didn't happen.

(E) is Out of Scope, too. What the study participants knew about the study does not explain why the bedding was ineffective.

2. (A) Flaw

Step 1: Identify the Question Type

The question directly asks why the argument is *flawed*, making this a Flaw question.

Step 2: Untangle the Stimulus

The author provides a lot of statistics about the hair dryers sold by Wilson. Five years ago, half the hair dryers sold in the country were Wilsons. Now, only 25% of the hair dryers sold are Wilsons. Wilson still makes the same amount of money per hair dryer sold, so the author concludes that Wilson's total hair dryer income has decreased.

Step 3: Make a Prediction

The conclusion is about total income. For total income to decrease, Wilson must take in less money overall. They are making the same amount of income on each hair dryer, so that means they would have to be selling fewer hair dryers overall. However, the evidence merely indicates that Wilson's hair dryers make up a smaller *percentage* of total hair dryers sold. If people started buying a lot more hair dryers overall, Wilson could still sell just as many or even more hair dryers despite making up a smaller percentage (i.e., share) of the market. (For example, 50% of 10,000 hair dryers is still as much as 25% of 20,000 hair dryers.) The author confuses numbers and percentages. The correct answer will point out this overlooked distinction.

Step 4: Evaluate the Answer Choices

(A) matches the prediction, pointing out the confusion between percentages (market share) and numbers (total sales). If total sales nationwide increase enough, a loss of market share does not have to indicate a loss in total sales.

(B) is Out of Scope. The argument is about income and market share. Information about how profits are generated is unnecessary.

(C) is Out of Scope. The conclusion and the entire argument is solely about hair dryer sales. Sales for other products have no bearing on that.

(D) is also Out of Scope. Even if the retail price increased (i.e., the amount you'd pay in the store), Wilson is still said to receive the same *net* income per hair dryer. Given that *net* income hasn't changed, an increase in retail price just means that extra money is going somewhere else. Perhaps the cost of making each hair dryer has also gone up, or perhaps the stores are making more money per hair dryer, not Wilson.

(E) is Extreme and Out of Scope. It doesn't matter how Wilson's hair dryers compare to its other products. Besides, the author isn't trying to argue that the hair dryers are the *least* profitable.

3. (A) Main Point

Step 1: Identify the Question Type

The question asks for the "overall conclusion" of the argument, making this a Main Point question.

Step 2: Untangle the Stimulus

The argument is riddled with a bunch of philosophical buzzwords. To cut through the muck, it helps to paraphrase it in a more conversational tone: "Is being faithful a virtue? It depends on what you're faithful to. You see, virtues are supposed to be good. But resentment is a type of faithfulness, and resentment is no virtue because it means being faithful to bad things."

Step 3: Make a Prediction

So what's the point of all this? The author is ultimately trying to answer the question of whether faithfulness can be considered a virtue. The answer? That's the conclusion: it depends on what you're faithful to. Everything else is just evidence to support that point.

Step 4: Evaluate the Answer Choices

(A) is a clean paraphrase of the opening sentence, which sums up the author's conclusion.

(B) is a given fact, and facts are evidence. The fact that virtues are, by definition, praiseworthy is evidence why the author argues that faithfulness is not always a virtue.

(C) can be inferred, but is not the main point. The author does suggest that hate-based behavior (resentment) is not virtuous, but that's just evidence why faithfulness is not always virtuous.

(D) is a 180. The author claims that resentment is *in fact* a kind of faithfulness. There is no suggestion that they are "obviously different."

(E) is a Distortion. The author claims that nobody considers resentment virtuous, but never actually claims that this *should* be the case. Besides, the status of resentment is merely evidence for why faithfulness as a virtue depends on other factors.

4. (E) Principle (Identify/Strengthen)

Step 1: Identify the Question Type

The question directly asks for a principle. Because the principle will be listed in the answer choices, this is an Identify the Principle question. Further, because the correct answer will help "justify the columnist's judgment," it will also act like a Strengthen question.

Step 2: Untangle the Stimulus

The columnist's judgment comes in the last sentence: "That proposal is unacceptable." The disputed proposal involves taking additional water utility revenue and using it to build new roads instead of a new dam, as was originally the plan.

Step 3: Make a Prediction

Specifically, the columnist is rejecting a proposal, claiming it's unacceptable to take money collected by a water utility and use it to build something entirely unrelated: roads. The correct answer will justify this reasoning using the same logic, only in broader terms. In other words, something along the lines of: don't take money from one business and use it to build something unrelated to that business.

Step 4: Evaluate the Answer Choices

(E) matches the columnist's logic. If the water utility's additional charges need to be used for water-related expenses, then that justifies the columnist's argument against using those charges to build new roads.

(A) doesn't help. By this principle, as long as people know the money is going to be used for new roads, then there's no justification for calling the proposal unacceptable.

(B) is Out of Scope. There's no suggestion that a dam would benefit the entire community and/or that the new roads would only benefit some members.

(C) is Out of Scope. There's no information whether or not the customers approve of the proposal, so this offers no justification for the columnist's claim.

(D) is a Distortion. The argument is about how to use the revenue earned from the additional charges. It's never said who approved the additional charges in the first place, and the columnist is not arguing about who should or shouldn't approve those decisions.

5. (A) Assumption (Necessary)

Step 1: Identify the Question Type

The question directly asks for the assumption in the argument. The assumption is *required*, making this a Necessary Assumption question.

Step 2: Untangle the Stimulus

The final sentence offers a common "[s]ince [evidence], [conclusion]" format. The author concludes that the leopard magpie moth may become extinct. The evidence is that a plant called the Natal grass cycad is also going extinct. The moth eats this plant, which provides the moth with a predator-avoiding chemical.

Step 3: Make a Prediction

The loss of the cycad would certainly take away a source of protection for the moth. However, the author fails to consider that there just might be other sources of the helpful toxin the cycad produces. Moreover, even if other sources don't exist, the moth could still adapt and find a new way to avoid predators. The author assumes none of this will happen—that the cycad is the moth's *only* source of protection against predators.

Step 4: Evaluate the Answer Choices

(A) matches the prediction and must be assumed. After all, if there *were* other ways to become unpalatable to predators, then the extinction of the cycad would not necessarily spell doom for the moth.

(B) could help the author out, but is ultimately not necessary. Even if the moth *was* fast enough to escape predators, it could still face extinction by losing a crucial food source. This fails to make a needed connection between the cycad and the moth.

(C) is not necessary. It doesn't matter *how* predators sense the macrozamin. Whether they do sense it from appearance alone or by other means, the author still has a point.

(D) is not necessary. The moths don't need the plant to be abundant to be affected by the plant's impending extinction. Even if the moths could locate the plant at its rarest, that will be of no help should the plant disappear entirely.

(E) is Out of Scope and a 180 at worst. It may weaken the argument, because if the predators are not becoming immune that actually *helps* the magpie's chances. However, if the cycad disappears and macrozamin goes away, then it makes no difference whether the predators grow tolerant of it or not.

6. (B) Main Point

Step 1: Identify the Question Type

The question asks for the "conclusion drawn," making this a Main Point question.

Step 2: Untangle the Stimulus

The citizen uses a very common argumentative technique here: present someone else's point of view and refute it. In this case, the citizen's leaders believe that the government should use the budget surplus to pay down the national debt. The line "[t]his makes no sense" indicates the citizen's rebuttal, and thus the conclusion: the government should *not* use the surplus to pay down the debt. Everything else, including the list of other potential uses (the military, infrastructure, roads) and the analogy of homeowners paying off a mortgage, is merely evidence to back up the citizen's rebuttal.

Step 3: Make a Prediction

As often happens when an author rebuts a point of view, the rebuttal serves as the main point. Here, the citizen's conclusion is that, contrary to what the leaders suggest, the government should not use the budget surplus to pay down the national debt.

Step 4: Evaluate the Answer Choices

(B) accurately expresses the citizen's rebuttal and thus the main conclusion.

(A) takes the citizen's analogy and turns it into a recommendation. The citizen never directly states that homeowners shouldn't do this—and that's not the point. The analogy is there to argue why the government should not use the surplus to pay off the national debt.

(C) accurately expresses the citizen's belief that a homeowner's situation parallels the government's situation. However, that's merely evidence to support the citizen's

rebuttal of the leaders' view of what should be done with the budget surplus.

(D) brings up a detail that implies where the budget surplus could be better spent, but misses the bigger picture that the surplus *shouldn't* be used to pay down the national debt.

(E) accurately sums up the leaders' position, but completely misses the citizen's point that this plan "makes no sense."

7. (D) Point at Issue

Step 1: Identify the Question Type

There are two speakers, and the question asks for something about which the two speakers *disagree*. That indicates a Point at Issue question.

Step 2: Untangle the Stimulus

Peraski argues that people with small cars cannot complain about people with larger gas-guzzling cars causing pollution. After all, people with small cars could produce less pollution by riding a bike, so complaining about others would be hypocritical.

Jackson concedes that people could always be better about reducing pollution. However, Jackson is okay with being hypocritical if it means speaking out against people who are even worse.

Step 3: Make a Prediction

Both speakers acknowledge that people who pollute less can be hypocritical because they're still polluting. However, they differ in their feeling toward that hypocrisy. Peraski sees hypocrisy as a reason to stay quiet. Jackson, on the other hand, does not. To Jackson, hypocrisy is no excuse for staying quiet. The correct answer will address this argument about the role of hypocrisy.

Step 4: Evaluate the Answer Choices

(D) expresses the Point at Issue. Peraski would disagree with this statement; people should *not* speak out if it reveals hypocrisy. Jackson says the opposite: people *should* speak out, despite the hypocrisy.

(A) is a 180. Peraski directly states this, but Jackson would agree. They're not arguing about the level of pollution. They're arguing over whether people should speak out about it.

(B) is a 180. Both Peraski and Jackson agree that it would reveal hypocrisy. Their disagreement is about whether or not people should speak out in light of this hypocrisy.

(C) is also a 180. Peraski implies this directly, and Jackson would not disagree. The question is this: should these drivers of small cars speak out against pollution or not?

(E) is Out of Scope. Neither speaker addresses the concept of morality, so there's no way to know whether they would agree on this or not.

8. (C) Paradox

Step 1: Identify the Question Type

The question asks for something that would "resolve the apparent discrepancy," making this a Paradox question.

Step 2: Untangle the Stimulus

For a Paradox question, look for the central mystery. In this case, abalones become large only when they can spend more energy on mating and less energy finding food and avoiding predators. However, there's one species that became large after predators (otters) moved into their waters.

Step 3: Make a Prediction

If abalones need to spend less energy avoiding predators, how did this one species get bigger after *more* predators showed up? Perhaps something made it easy to avoid the otters, and thus their appearance was uneventful. There's another key to the mystery: abalones also need to spend less energy finding food. Perhaps the otters made it easier for the abalones to find food. The correct answer will likely draw on one or both of these potential solutions that helped the abalones out.

Step 4: Evaluate the Answer Choices

(C) is helpful on two accounts. First, it suggests that otters were eating something other than just abalones. Thus, the abalones didn't necessarily have to spend as much or more energy avoiding the otters because the otters were eating other creatures. Second, the otters were eating the abalones' competition for food, so the abalones didn't need as much energy to find food. Those are the exact conditions needed to help explain the presence of large abalones.

(A) is a 180. If the abalones and the otters compete for the same food, then the appearance of otters would have made it *harder* for the abalones to find food. That would make it *less* likely that they grew so large.

(B) is Out of Scope. It doesn't matter how many species exist. This still doesn't explain how they got large in the presence of predators.

(D) is Out of Scope. Reproductive ability is not presented as a factor in determining the size of the abalones.

(E) is also Out of Scope. The abalones developed to be larger *after* the otters showed up.

9. (D) Assumption (Sufficient)

Step 1: Identify the Question Type

This is an Assumption question, as it asks for something that is assumed. Further, the argument's conclusion can be properly drawn *if* that assumption is in place, making this a Sufficient Assumption question.

Step 2: Untangle the Stimulus

Managers encourage stiff competition among employees in the hopes that it will make employees perform their best. However, the author concludes ([t]*hus*) that stiff competition will actually make things worse. The evidence is that some people may become anxious and doubt their own abilities when faced with competition.

Step 3: Make a Prediction

The author makes a subtle shift in scope. Both the evidence and conclusion refer to the effect of stiff competition. However, the evidence merely claims it makes people anxious and doubtful of their abilities, while the conclusion shifts to claim it affects people's actual performance. The author is assuming there's a connection between anxiety/doubt and how people actually perform.

Step 4: Evaluate the Answer Choices

(D) makes the logical connection between doubt and one's actual performance. If this were true, then the author's argument is complete: stiff competition leads to doubt, and thus impacts performance.

(A) might explain why people doubt their abilities in the face of superior competition, but that still doesn't provide a logical connection to the conclusion, which is about actual performance.

(B) is Out of Scope. The goal is not about getting everyone to perform at the same level. The goal is to maximize performance for each employee individually. Even if the winner of a competition gives the most effort, the other employees could still be giving their own individual best effort, contrary to the author's conclusion.

(C) is a Distortion. This states that, when people feel they can win a competition, they will perform better. That doesn't mean, as the author suggests, that they *won't* perform better when they *don't* think they can win. Perhaps the competition itself is enough to motivate performance.

(E) is Out of Scope. It indicates why some people might be anxious or doubtful, but it still does not make a logical connection to the conclusion, which is about actual performance.

10. (D) Inference

Step 1: Identify the Question Type

Grounds for choosing the correct answer will be made "on the basis of the statements above." That makes this an Inference question. However, unlike most Inference questions, the correct answer will not be true or supported as valid. The correct answer will be *rejected*, which means the stimulus will be used to contradict the correct answer—it must be false. Answer choices that could be true or must be true can be rejected.

Step 2: Untangle the Stimulus

The stimulus merely provides details explaining the difficulty of creating a database of every known plant species. Not only do botanists sometimes give the same plant different names (because they didn't know someone else already named it), but also DNA shows how they sometimes use the same name for plants that are actually different.

Step 3: Make a Prediction

Those wacky botanists, with such convoluted records—different plants with the same name, the same plant with different names—it's no wonder that creating a database is so complicated. However, what does this imply? What does it counter? It's almost impossible to predict. With so little to work with, there's no choice but to test each answer individually with the information given. Remember that the correct answer will be directly contradicted by what's provided.

Step 4: Evaluate the Answer Choices

(D) can be rejected. The last sentence directly states how DNA analysis can be used to identify different species. That technique could be used to identify different species, whether those species were given the same name or distinct ones. So, contrary to this claim, the botanists *do* have a viable technique.

(A) is not supported, but it can't be rejected either. There's no indication of how many problems have been identified or how many of those problems have yet to be resolved. It's still possible that *most* inconsistencies are still being worked out.

(B) certainly cannot be rejected. While it hasn't been easy to create, there must be a reason they're trying. Therefore, it's actually very likely that the database would be helpful.

(C) cannot be rejected. While the stimulus only refers to these issues in botany, there's no reason to believe similar issues aren't happening elsewhere.

(E) cannot be rejected. If a plant has multiple names, that could mean multiple botanists discovered information about it. Only searching for information under one name could easily leave out information collected by a botanist who gave it a different name.

11. (D) Strengthen

Step 1: Identify the Question Type

The question directly asks for something that strengthens the given argument.

Step 2: Untangle the Stimulus

The author concludes ([c]*learly*) that the knowledge of being monitored causes hospital staff to perform their work more carefully. The evidence is that there were fewer injuries caused by staff error after a program was implemented to record such errors.

Step 3: Make a Prediction

There are two problems with the argument. The first is one of the most common flaws tested on the LSAT: causation versus correlation. The evidence merely describes a correlation (errors decreased at the same time the program was implemented). The conclusion claims one thing caused the other (the monitoring program *caused* people to make fewer errors). The second problem involves a scope shift. The evidence claims that the program involved *recording* errors, but the conclusion only discusses the knowledge of being monitored. The author fails to consider that it wasn't the monitoring but rather the actual recording of errors that made people more careful. To combat these weaknesses and make the argument stronger, the correct answer will strengthen the connection between the program and the decreased number of errors and/or make it more likely that it was the monitoring and not necessarily the recordkeeping itself.

Step 4: Evaluate the Answer Choices

(D) strengthens the argument by addressing both weaknesses. This strengthens the connection between the plan and the decreased errors by showing how errors weren't decreasing earlier. That rules out earlier causes and makes the monitoring program a more likely cause. It also makes it clearer that it's the analysis (i.e., monitoring) of the records that people noticed.

(A) is a 180. This suggests that monitoring was nothing new, making it more likely that people were concerned about some other aspect of the program. Perhaps they were always monitored, but nothing was ever recorded before and people are now nervous about having a physical record of their mistakes.

(B) is a 180. This suggests that patient errors decreased elsewhere *without* the plan. That implies there was another cause entirely.

(C) is Out of Scope. What the plan does *not* involve provides no support for whether or not the plan was responsible for changing people's behavior.

(E) is Out of Scope. It doesn't matter what the punishment is when people *did* make an error. The argument is about what caused people to make *fewer* errors. If anything, a discussion of penalties (reprimands or otherwise) could provide an alternative cause for better behavior.

12. (C) Paradox

Step 1: Identify the Question Type

The question asks for something that "helps to explain" a situation. If a situation needs explaining, that indicates a Paradox question.

Step 2: Untangle the Stimulus

In a certain area, wolves were introduced to reduce the growing moose population. Contrary to expectations, despite a healthy wolf population, the moose population actually kept growing.

Step 3: Make a Prediction

If the wolf population is doing well, why didn't they stop the moose population from growing? While it may be difficult to predict an exact solution, expect that the correct answer will show how the wolves created an unexpected benefit.

Step 4: Evaluate the Answer Choices

(C) provides an explanation. Without the wolves, the moose were susceptible to diseases that could have killed them off. With the wolves, the disease-weakened moose are picked off, preventing the disease from spreading and thus giving the moose a better chance of staying healthy and surviving.

(A) may be tempting in that it suggests that moose predators were kept away by the wolves, helping the moose to survive. However, the other predators were still replaced by wolves, who also prey on moose. This only works if wolves are a lesser threat. However, that information is not provided, and the correct answer cannot depend on an unsubstantiated condition.

(B) tries to suggest that the mystery is not all that unusual. Other parks have the same problem. However, this still fails to explain *why* that problem exists in the first place. So essentially, this only makes matters worse by expanding the mystery to other areas.

(D) is an Irrelevant Comparison. The eating habits of a healthy moose versus unhealthy moose does nothing to explain why wolves had no effect on the moose population.

(E) is an Irrelevant Comparison. It doesn't help because it's restricted to old moose. This might explain why wolves don't affect the population of *old* moose—they'd be just as likely to die without the wolves around—but it doesn't explain why wolves had no effect on the *overall* moose population.

13. (A) Flaw

Step 1: Identify the Question Type

The question asks why the argument is *flawed*, making this easily identified as a Flaw question.

Step 2: Untangle the Stimulus

The conclusion ([*h*]*ence*) is that, if laws are not meant to make people happy, then existing laws cannot be evaluated and are thus considered legitimate just for being laws. The evidence is that, if laws *are* meant to make people happy, then existing laws *could* be criticized (i.e., evaluated).

Conclusion:

If	*purpose is* *~ happiness*	→	*~ basis for* *evaluation/criticism*

Evidence:

If	*purpose is* *happiness*	→	*basis for evaluation/* *criticism*

Step 3: Make a Prediction

Few things are greater on the LSAT than finding an argument in which the evidence and conclusion both consist of Formal Logic. That's often a sign of a commonly tested flaw: necessity versus sufficiency. Sure enough, the evidence claims that *if* the purpose of laws was to make people happy, that would be good enough (i.e., sufficient) to allow for critique of existing laws. However, the author suggests that we can't critique existing laws if that's *not* the purpose—as if making people happy had to be the purpose (i.e., was necessary). That's not necessarily true. It's possible that critiques are valid whatever the purpose is. The correct answer will point out this common flaw of treating a sufficient condition as if it were necessary.

Step 4: Evaluate the Answer Choices

(A) points out the common flaw being tested here. The author takes a sufficient condition (i.e., *if* the purpose of laws is to make people happy) and treats it as necessary (i.e., we can't evaluate laws without that purpose).

(B) brings up another commonly tested flaw: causation versus correlation. However, the author is not suggesting that anything caused anything else, so this flaw does not apply here.

(C) describes the flaw of equivocation (treating two different concepts as equal just because the same word is used to describe them). However, all terms are used consistently in the argument, so equivocation is not a problem here.

(D) suggests that the evidence is about how the world *should* be, but the author never makes such a claim.

(E) describes a flaw in which the evidence is about a group as a whole and the conclusion is about individual members within that group. However, there is no group here from which individual members are identified.

14. (C) Parallel Reasoning

Step 1: Identify the Question Type

The question asks for an argument "most similar to" the argument in the stimulus. That makes this a Parallel Reasoning question.

Step 2: Untangle the Stimulus

The author concludes there is no life on planet P23. The evidence is that water on the surface is required for life, and planet P23 has no water on the surface.

Step 3: Make a Prediction

The structure here uses some very fundamental Formal Logic. In order for an event to occur (life), there's a requirement (water). That requirement isn't met, so the event won't happen. Essentially, it's an argument based on employing the contrapositive:

If	life	$\rightarrow$	water
If	~ water	$\rightarrow$	~ life

The correct answer will use the exact same logical structure.

Step 4: Evaluate the Answer Choices

(C) is a match, employing the contrapositive exactly like the original argument. For an event to occur (increase drilling), there's a requirement (new equipment). That requirement is not met, so the author concludes the event won't happen.

If	increasing drilling	$\rightarrow$	new equipment
If	~ new equipment	$\rightarrow$	~ increasing drilling

(A) presents too many variables. It starts with a requirement for success (efficiency). However, the author suggests that certain employees *probably* have that requirement and then illogically concludes that such employees are needed. In addition to being illogical, this does not match the original structure of *not* meeting a requirement.

(B) is too wishy-washy with what "might be" true or is "not necessarily" true. The original argument was far more absolute. Furthermore, there is no requirement that goes unmet here.

(D) uses Formal Logic, but makes a crucial error. In this case, there is a requirement (real estate prices increase) for an event to occur (improve economy). However, this argument says the requirement *is* met, and concludes the event *is* happening. Not only is that improper Formal Logic (treating a necessary condition as if it were sufficient), but it doesn't match the original logic, which involves the requirement *not* being met.

(E) properly uses Formal Logic, but not in the same way as the original argument. Here, when one event happens (exports decrease), a result occurs (trade deficit increases). The event *does* happen, so the author concludes the result *does* occur. The logic works, but it does not employ the contrapositive based on a requirement *not* being met.

15. (C) Point at Issue

Step 1: Identify the Question Type

There are two speakers, and the question asks for something about which the speakers *disagree*. That makes this a Point at Issue question.

Step 2: Untangle the Stimulus

Sanchez argues that the school did not spend too much money on new computers because the computers were actually cheaper than assumed. Merriweather isn't concerned that the school got a good deal. The problem is that the computers were too elaborate.

Step 3: Make a Prediction

Merriweather is not disputing the fact that the computers were fairly priced. Merriweather is disputing the claim about overspending, suggesting the school *did* pay too much—not because the computers were overly expensive, but because they were unnecessarily elaborate. The correct answer will address the debate over whether the school spent more than it needed.

Step 4: Evaluate the Answer Choices

(C) describes the Point at Issue. Sanchez claims the school did *not* spend more than it should. Merriweather implies that it *did*.

(A) is a Distortion. Merriweather does not dispute the need for new computers. Merriweather merely has an issue with the particular computers purchased.

(B) is a Distortion. Merriweather is not disputing the *number* of computers purchased. Merriweather is disputing the *type* of computers purchased.

(D) is a 180. Sanchez implies that the price for that particular computer was not too high, and Merriweather *agrees*, suggesting that's not the issue. It's not about whether the school got a good deal on that particular computer model, it's about the computers purchased being unnecessarily elaborate.

(E) is Extreme and Out of Scope, as Sanchez never suggests the school was *harshly* criticized. Also, Merriweather does not address how other people reacted to the purchase.

16. (B) Flaw

Step 1: Identify the Question Type

The question directly asks for the flaw in the argument.

Step 2: Untangle the Stimulus

The argument starts with two sets of statistics. The administrator claims that only 1 in 2,000,000 flights veer off course when landing. Opponents suggest the situation is worse, claiming 1 in 20,000 flights veer off course. The administrator concludes (*so*) that the opponents' statistics are less reliable. The evidence is that the opponents' statistics are based on a partial review of air traffic control tapes while the administrator's statistics are based on a complete review of pilot reports.

Step 3: Make a Prediction

The administrator has a point about the opponents using partial data. However, the administrator overlooks a potentially more significant difference: the source of the statistics. The opponents reviewed air traffic control tapes. The administrator reviewed reports from pilots. The administrator assumes that pilot reports are just as reliable, if not more reliable, than air traffic control tapes. The correct answer will describe why this might not be valid.

Step 4: Evaluate the Answer Choices

(B) describes the flaw. The administrator assumes the pilot reports are more reliable. However, when a plane veers off course, that's often a pilot error. If pilots are reluctant to report those mistakes, that brings the administrator's entire argument into question.

(A) is Out of Scope. The argument is about the reliability of the statistics, not what would happen if the runways are built closer together.

(C) is not supported. The administrator makes no attack on the opponents' motives or integrity.

(D) is a Distortion. The administrator does not suggest the air traffic control tapes are inaccurate. The administrator merely suggests that the opponents did not see everything. Perhaps the opponents only saw an unrepresentative sample of tapes.

(E) is Extreme. The airport administrator never suggests the opponents' statistics *must* be inaccurate. Besides, the administrator doesn't question the accuracy. The administrator merely implies that the statistics are based on an incomplete review. The results are accurate, but don't represent the whole picture.

17. (E) Assumption (Necessary)

Step 1: Identify the Question Type

The question directly asks for an assumption, and one on which the argument *depends*. That makes this a Necessary Assumption question.

Step 2: Untangle the Stimulus

The author concludes ([*s*]*o*) that, when lakes are partially iced over, anglers are better off looking for trout in shallower water. The evidence is that trout generally swim in colder water. In the summer, water is colder at the bottom, and in the winter, water is colder at the top. "Turnover" occurs in the fall, bringing colder water to the surface. Then, "turnover" occurs again in late winter, bringing colder water back to the bottom.

Step 3: Make a Prediction

The colder water (which trout prefer) is near the surface during the winter, after the water turns in the fall and before it turns back in the late winter. The author's argument, however, is based on when the lake is "partially iced over." The author must assume that the ice indicates that the water is still colder near the surface, and thus the water hasn't had its end-of-winter "turnover" yet.

Step 4: Evaluate the Answer Choices

(E) must be assumed. After all, if the late-winter "turnover" *had* occurred, then the water would be colder on the bottom despite the appearance of ice on the surface. In that case, the author has no reason to recommend shallow waters. The author must assume the "turnover" has not occurred yet.

(A) is Out of Scope. The author is never suggesting or assuming that catching trout is any *easier* at any given time of the year. The only difference is where they're likely to be found.

(B) is Out of Scope. The argument is about finding trout, and there's no indication that density plays any role in determining where the trout are.

(C) is Extreme. The author's argument is about where to find trout in deep temperate lakes, but there's no suggestion that lake trout couldn't be found in other lakes.

(D) is Out of Scope. The argument is based solely on *where* the trout are found, not *how* they feed.

18. (D) Point at Issue (Agree)

Step 1: Identify the Question Type

This is a Point at Issue question, as it asks for something supported by the argument between two speakers. However, unlike most Point at Issue questions, this asks for something with which the authors *agree*, as opposed to the usual point of disagreement.

Step 2: Untangle the Stimulus

Liang argues that children should not watch violent movies because such movies make viewers more aggressive. Sarah counters that violent movies are okay for mature audiences because such movies help people purge their aggressive emotions.

Step 3: Make a Prediction

If this were a standard Point at Issue question, the disagreement would be clear: Liang wants to restrict access to violent movies while Sarah is okay with them (even if they are referring to different audiences). Their arguments are so contrasting that it's hard to find a point of agreement. If there's anything to predict here, it's that they both agree that violent movies can have *some* effect on people, even if they don't quite agree on what that effect is. Just anticipate that the correct answer will likely be vague, as Liang and Sarah tend to disagree on a lot of the specific details.

Step 4: Evaluate the Answer Choices

(D) is a point of agreement. Liang believes violent movies have some effect (they make people more aggressive), and so does Sarah (they help people purge emotions). They may disagree on the actual effect, but they do agree there is *some* understanding of how viewers are affected.

(A) is a 180. Sarah directly claims that movies allow viewers to purge their aggression, while Liang argues that movies make people *more* aggressive. This would be a great answer to a more standard Point at Issue question, which is why it's important to read question stems carefully.

(B) is Out of Scope. Liang doesn't address mature audiences, and Sarah never discusses what mature audiences believe is acceptable.

(C) is unsupported. Liang clearly agrees with this. However, Sarah doesn't believe that violent movies cause violence in viewers. Because of that, there's no way to know how Sarah would react if she *did* believe that were true.

(E) is an Irrelevant Comparison. Neither author makes a direct comparison between children and adults, let alone who is more attracted to violent movies.

19. (A) Weaken

Step 1: Identify the Question Type

The question asks for something that "casts the most doubt" on the given argument. That makes this a Weaken question.

Step 2: Untangle the Stimulus

The politician leads right off with the conclusion: Thompson is the best candidate to lead the nation. The evidence is that Thompson is the only candidate who opposes higher taxes, a sign that most people would agree points to good leadership.

Step 3: Make a Prediction

The entire argument rests on Thompson's opposition to higher taxes—as if opposing higher taxes was the *only* significant factor in determining who's the best leader. Quite simply, this argument could be weakened by showing that opposition to higher taxes is insignificant.

Step 4: Evaluate the Answer Choices

(A) makes a direct attack. If opposing higher taxes is not a factor, then the politician's entire argument in favor of Thompson is shot.

(B) may be quite tempting, as it seems to sever the link between opposing higher taxes and being a good leader. However, this merely claims that opposing higher taxes is not *sufficient*, i.e., it's not enough by itself to guarantee good leadership. However, the politician isn't suggesting that it's enough by itself. The politician is implying that it's important or even necessary. Even if it's not sufficient, the politician could still have a point by saying it's necessary, and Thompson is the only candidate to meet that requirement.

(C) is Out of Scope. It's possible that the other candidates have equally questionable opinions on other issues. In addition, the politician could still claim that taxes are more significant than those issues. Without more information, this does not affect the politician's argument.

(D) is Out of Scope. Even if people who supported higher taxes were adequate leaders (not exactly a ringing endorsement), Thompson could still be better.

(E) is also Out of Scope. The politician is not making any claims or suggestions about people's work ethic. The argument is solely about what makes a good leader.

20. (A) Method of Argument

Step 1: Identify the Question Type

The phrase "by doing which of the following" indicates that the question is asking for *how* Garza responds as opposed to *what* Garza says. That makes this a Method of Argument question.

Step 2: Untangle the Stimulus

Patterson argues that music most likely arose during the Upper Paleolithic period because that's the source of the earliest known evidence of music: bone flutes. Garza points out that bone just happens to survive better in archaeological environments than other materials.

Step 3: Make a Prediction

Garza never comes out and claims Patterson is wrong. However, Garza implies that the evidence of bone flutes is perhaps not as conclusive as Patterson believes. There may have been earlier instruments that just didn't survive. The correct answer will describe Garza's questioning of

Patterson's argument by suggesting that the evidence is inconclusive.

Step 4: Evaluate the Answer Choices

(A) describes Garza's method. Garza argues that Patterson's evidence about bone flutes may not be enough to fully support Patterson's claim about when music arose.

(B) is inaccurate. Garza does not attack the premise (i.e., evidence) behind Patterson's argument. The bone flutes *are* the earliest evidence we have of music. Garza merely raises the point that there may be other evidence we don't know about because it didn't survive.

(C) is a Distortion. Garza does not present any evidence that directly counters Patterson's claim. Garza merely suggests that Patterson's claim *may* not be fully supported.

(D) is not accurate. Garza does not draw any analogy. If anything, the comparison Garza draws between bone and other materials suggests they are *not* analogous.

(E) is not accurate. Garza provides distinct evidence and never actually draws a conclusion in contrast to Patterson. Everything in Garza's argument merely *implies* that Patterson may have overlooked something.

21. (B) Principle (Apply/Inference)

Step 1: Identify the Question Type

The correct answer will be a specific argument that is justified by a principle given in the stimulus. That makes this an Apply the Principle question.

Step 2: Untangle the Stimulus

The principle given consists of a single piece of Formal Logic: No job should require a license unless people are at risk if the job goes wrong.

Step 3: Make a Prediction

The key to this question is to translate the Formal Logic properly. In order to require a license, there must be a risk to others. By contrapositive, if there is no risk, then there's no need to require a license.

| *If* | *require license* | → | *risk* |
| *If* | *~ risk* | → | *~ license required* |

Note that the risk to others is a *necessary* condition. There *needs* to be a risk to require a license. That does not mean that a risk to others is *sufficient*. In other words, even if people are at risk, the principle does not state that a license must be required. Expect this to be a trap in at least one answer. The correct answer must conform to the proper Formal Logic. Also note that the risk must come from tasks *normally* carried out in the job.

Step 4: Evaluate the Answer Choices

(B) conforms to the logic. In this case, there is no realistic risk if an interior designer makes a mistake, so no license need be required.

(A) is a Distortion. It only claims that *some* duties carry no risk. However, those might be uncommon duties. It's still possible (and probable) that most other duties *do* carry risks if done improperly, and thus a license *could* be required.

(C) gets the logic backward. To require a license, there *must* be risk to others. However, that doesn't mean any job that carries a risk *must* require a license.

(D) also gets the logic backward. To require a license, there *must* be risk to others. However, that doesn't mean any job that carries a risk *must* require a license.

(E), just like **(C)** and **(D)**, gets the logic backward. To require a license, there *must* be risk to others. However, that doesn't mean any job that carries a risk *must* require a license.

22. (D) Inference

Step 1: Identify the Question Type

The question asks for something that "must be true" based on the given information. That makes this an Inference question.

Step 2: Untangle the Stimulus

The author presents three statistics: 1) most cars sold last year by Regis Motors were sold to Blomenville residents, 2) Regis Motors sold more cars last year than in any year before that, and 3) most cars sold last year to Blomenville residents were not from Regis Motors.

Step 3: Make a Prediction

Start with that middle statistic: last year, Regis Motors had a record-setting year. How many more cars did Regis Motors sell than in previous years? Where were those cars sold in previous years? Nobody knows the answer to these questions. There are no deductions to glean from this statistic, so it's unlikely to have anything to do with the correct answer.

The surrounding sentences, on the other hand, both refer to sales in Blomenville. Last year, cars from Regis made up less than half the sales to Blomenville residents. That means the total number of cars sold in Blomenville was more than twice as much as cars sold there by Regis alone. In addition, the number of cars Regis sold in Blomenville comprises most (more than 50%) of Regis's total sales. Putting those figures together, the total number of cars sold in Blomenville was over twice as much as most of Regis's overall sales. In other words, the total number of cars sold in Blomenville was more than 100% of Regis's overall sale. More cars were sold overall in Blomenville than Regis's entire output for the year.

If the math is too complex, picking some simple numbers can help clear it up. For example, say Regis sold 1,000 cars overall. Then at least 501 of them were sold in Blomenville. However, that's less than half the sales in Blomenville. So at least 1,003 cars were sold in Blomenville—more than all the cars sold by Regis. This is a question worth skipping if the numbers are too much to manage. Otherwise, test the answers one at a time, and eliminate ones that are clearly unsupported.

Step 4: Evaluate the Answer Choices

(D) must be true. The total sales in Blomenville were at least double the sales by Regis in Blomenville, and sales in Blomenville made up most (>50%) of Regis's overall sales. That means total sales in Blomenville were more than 100% of Regis's overall sales.

(A) is not supported. The only comparison from last year to previous years is the total number of cars sold by Regis overall. There's no way to know where those cars were sold in the past. It's possible that Regis expanded into other areas last year and increased its total sales by selling to other regions, while not making any change to its sales in Blomenville.

(B) is not supported. There is no information provided to compare sales in Blomenville from one year to the next. The only information provided about multiple years refers solely to Regis's overall sales.

(C) may be tempting, but is not supported. While most cars in Blomenville were sold to other companies, there does not have to be one particular retailer that surpassed Regis. It's possible that Regis sold just 100 cars there and 500 cars were sold by 10 other retailers who sold just 50 cars each. In that case, Regis is still the winner by a long shot.

(E) is not supported. The only mention of previous years refers exclusively to Regis's overall sales. It's possible that Regis was the only retailer in Blomenville until last year when new companies came in and cut into Regis's share.

23. (E) Strengthen

Step 1: Identify the Question Type

The question asks for something that "provides the most support" for the given argument. That means it will strengthen that argument.

Step 2: Untangle the Stimulus

The editorial's author concludes that starting school after 8:00 A.M. can reduce the number of accidents involving teenagers driving to school. There are two pieces of evidence for this. The first is scientific: Students are sleepy if they wake up before 8:00 A.M. because their body is still producing melatonin. The second is anecdotal: The number of accidents

in Granville decreased after the school changed its start time to 8:30 A.M.

Step 3: Make a Prediction

The scientific evidence is pretty strong. The anecdotal evidence, on the other hand, contains a commonly tested flaw on the LSAT: causation versus correlation. The accident rate decreased during the same period that the school time was changed. However, the author implies that the later starting time of school was the *cause* of fewer accidents. This ignores other possible causes for the decrease in accidents. To combat this and thus strengthen the argument, the correct answer should reject alternate causes and/or provide more support for the link between later school starts and fewer accidents.

Step 4: Evaluate the Answer Choices

(E) strengthens the author's argument. If car accidents increased outside of Granville, that eliminates the possibility that Granville's rate was part of some regional trend. That doesn't *prove* that later start times were the cause, but it does eliminate other possible causes, thus making it more likely that the later start time was a factor.

(A) is an Irrelevant Comparison. The argument is only about teenagers, so it doesn't matter when younger children produce melatonin . . . unless *they* start driving to school—but that's another issue altogether.

(B) is Out of Scope. This may provide another reason why moving up the start time is a good idea, but tardiness has nothing to do with preventing car accidents.

(C) is an Irrelevant Comparison. The argument is only about preventing accidents as teenagers drive to school. Teenagers who work during the day have no bearing on the argument. Further, this talks about the amount of time one drives, which does not necessarily impact accident rates.

(D) is an Irrelevant Comparison. It doesn't matter what time of the day is more prone to accidents. The argument is merely focused on reducing accidents in the morning, and this offers no support that that will happen.

24. (E) Parallel Flaw

Step 1: Identify the Question Type

The correct answer will be an argument "most similar to" the one in the stimulus, and that reasoning is described as *flawed*. That makes this a Parallel Flaw question.

Step 2: Untangle the Stimulus

The author concludes that Lucinda will probably live in Western Hall. The evidence is that she's an engineering major, and most residents of Western Hall are engineering majors.

Step 3: Make a Prediction

The author misuses the logic of the term *most*. Just because most students in Western Hall are engineering majors doesn't mean most engineering majors are in Western Hall. It's possible that there are very few students in Western Hall to begin with and there a lot more engineering majors in other buildings, too. The correct answer will make the same misuse of the word *most*. The author will claim that most members of a group (Western Hall residents) possess a certain quality (engineering major) and then try to suggest that someone or something with that quality is likely to be part of that group.

Step 4: Evaluate the Answer Choices

(E) matches the logic and commits the same flaw. The author claims that most members of a group (hubs) possess a certain quality (mall) and then tries to suggest that a city with that quality is likely to become part of that group. Like the original author, this author fails to consider that there are very few hubs and there are probably a lot more malls in cities that aren't hubs.

(A) does not match and is actually more logical. Here, the author does claim that most members of a group (cities with a mall) possess a certain quality (hub). However, the author's city is now becoming part of that group, and the author reasonably suggests that it may possess the quality that most cities with a mall have.

(B) is an entirely different argument and is also more logical than the stimulus. If cities that are hubs *generally* experience something, and the city in question hasn't yet experienced it, then it is likely it *probably* will experience it in the future. Perhaps there are factors why it won't, but provided it is comparable to other hubs, the prediction that it *likely* will holds.

(C) does not match. For starters, it claims that members of a group (hubs) *always* possess a quality (excellent transportation)—which is already stronger language than that used by the original argument. Furthermore, the evidence is about what people *believe*, and they believe the city does *not* possess the quality mentioned. This is just not the same as the original.

(D) mixes up the evidence and the conclusion. The original used evidence of what was true for most students to draw a conclusion about one in particular. This argument uses evidence of one city to draw a conclusion about most cities. The logic is certainly flawed, but not in the same manner as the original.

25. (C) Assumption (Necessary)

Step 1: Identify the Question Type

The question directly asks for an assumption, and one that the argument *requires*. That makes this a Necessary Assumption question.

Step 2: Untangle the Stimulus

The oceanographer wants to reduce the amount of carbon dioxide in the atmosphere. So, the oceanographer makes a recommendation, which serves as the conclusion of the argument: pump the carbon dioxide deep into the ocean where it will dissolve in the water. The premise of this plan is that it takes hundreds of years for deeper, cooler water to mix with the warmer water. So long, carbon dioxide!

Step 3: Make a Prediction

It sounds like a great plan, but there's one little problem. The evidence claims that the *water* will take centuries to mix. However, it's possible that the carbon dioxide is less sluggish and can make its way up from the depths long before the cooler water decides to mix things up. The oceanographer must assume that once the carbon dioxide dissolves in the deep water, it will *stay* in the cool water until that water mixes upwards in a few centuries.

Step 4: Evaluate the Answer Choices

(C) must be assumed, claiming that carbon dioxide will not escape and will stay down in the depths until the cooler water mixes upwards. After all, if it *could* escape before that time, then the plan wouldn't quite work as intended.

(A) is not necessary. Even if it didn't dissolve very thoroughly, it could still dissolve enough to be trapped in the depths for centuries. The argument works with or without this claim.

(B) is Out of Scope. This is about carbon dioxide coming from evaporating water near the surface. However, it doesn't matter if this evaporating water releases a lot of carbon dioxide or not. Either way, the oceanographer's plan could still get rid of enough carbon dioxide in the atmosphere to make up for any additional carbon dioxide created by evaporation of the warmer water near the surface.

(D) is Extreme. The water may be denser, but it doesn't have to be the *main* reason carbon dioxide gets trapped. The argument would work equally well if temperature was the main factor.

(E) is Extreme. The oceanographer is not saying carbon dioxide *must* be trapped for hundreds of years to reduce its levels in the atmosphere. It's a plan, but it's not necessarily the only plan.

Section II: Reading Comprehension
Passage 1: John Rawls's Theory of Justice

Q#	Question Type	Correct	Difficulty
1	Detail	A	★
2	Logic Function	D	★
3	Global	B	★★
4	Inference	A	★★★★
5	Inference	E	★★★
6	Logic Reasoning (Weaken)	C	★★★★

Passage 2: The Great Migration

Q#	Question Type	Correct	Difficulty
7	Global	E	★
8	Detail	A	★
9	Logic Function	D	★
10	Inference	A	★★
11	Logic Function	D	★
12	Inference	C	★
13	Logic Reasoning (Strengthen)	B	★★

Passage 3: Insider Trading

Q#	Question Type	Correct	Difficulty
14	Global	D	★
15	Inference	B	★
16	Inference	C	★★★
17	Inference	E	★★
18	Logic Reasoning (Method of Arg.)	B	★★
19	Logic Function	D	★★★★

Passage 4: Brain Scans

Q#	Question Type	Correct	Difficulty
20	Global	B	★★
21	Detail	A	★
22	Inference	D	★★
23	Logic Function	E	★★★
24	Logic Function	A	★★★
25	Detail	E	★
26	Inference	C	★★★
27	Logic Reasoning (Parallel Reasoning)	B	★★★★

Passage 1: John Rawls's Theory of Justice

Step 1: Read the Passage Strategically

Sample Roadmap

line #	Keyword/phrase	¶ Margin notes
2	first needs; against	Utilitarian view:
3	dominant	maximize satisfaction
4	emphasized	Rawls: no reason to violate rights of few
6	At first; seems plausible	
8	but	
9	odd consequences; Suppose	
11	Incredibly	
13	accordingly; complains	
17	If; reject	Rawls: justice based on fairness
19	ingenious; asserts	
22	key	
23	:	
25	But	What's fair?
26	clever	Example: dividing cake
27	Suppose	
35	generalizes	General idea: ignorance ⸱⸱⸱⸱⸱⸱> ensure nobody loses ⸱⸱⸱⸱⸱⸱> just
44	thinks	Rawls: people want primary goods
49	Hence	Auth: some people still lose out
50	should	
51	Unfortunately	

Discussion

The passage seems to open mid-conversation, wasting no time with background information or filler. The author jumps right into the **Topic** (John Rawls's theory of justice), explaining how one needs context to understand it. The rest of the first paragraph provides that context: a description of utilitarianism, the dominant approach to justice that Rawls was reacting against. Utilitarianism is about doing what satisfies the greatest number of people, a concept that Rawls complains unfairly violates certain people's rights.

The second paragraph introduces Rawls's theory, presenting it as an alternative to utilitarianism. That makes it clearer that the **Scope** of the passage is how Rawls's theory counteracts utilitarianism and the **Purpose** is to describe how Rawls's theory works as an alternative. Instead of trying to satisfy as many people as possible, Rawls's idea (which the author refers to as *ingenious*) is that justice should be based on procedures agreed upon as fair.

In the third paragraph, the author raises a valid question: what constitutes fair? Rawls has an approach called the "veil of ignorance," which the author calls *clever*. The author presents an example involving a child dividing a cake, which merely serves to illustrate the general idea described in the fourth paragraph: people are self-serving, but they don't always know what they're going to get. Therefore, instead of risking a loss for the sake of getting the best outcome, they come up with a solution that ensures no complete loss because everybody gets something.

Rawls argues, in the last paragraph, that people will apply this theory to ensure they get "primary goods," such as rights, power, and money. Give everyone something, and nobody loses. Unfortunately, despite previous praise for Rawls's ideas, the author ultimately argues that Rawls's theory is flawed and will still lead to some people gaining at the expense of others. Thus, the **Main Idea** of the passage is that Rawls's veil of ignorance theory of justice offers a clever alternative to utilitarianism, but would still have a negative impact on some people.

1. (A) Detail

Step 2: Identify the Question Type

The question asks for something directly used and mentioned in the passage, making this a Detail question.

Step 3: Research the Relevant Text

Rawls's theory is explained generally in the fourth paragraph and illustrated with the cake scenario in the third paragraph.

Step 4: Make a Prediction

The theory is most clearly explained by the cake scenario described in the third paragraph. This scenario is referred to as a "thought experiment" in the fourth paragraph (line 36).

Step 5: Evaluate the Answer Choices

(A) is a direct match to the language of the passage.

(B) is a Distortion. Rawls rejects the theory of utilitarianism, but never uses any process of elimination to explain his own theory.

(C) mentions empirical studies, of which none are mentioned anywhere in the passage.

(D) is a Distortion. Rawls asserts that fairness can help people settle on a "principle of justice" (lines 21–22), but does not derive any deductions from such principles.

(E) mentions the meaning of words, which could only logically apply to Rawls's definition of "primary goods" in the last paragraph. However, that definition does not explain the theory itself.

2. (D) Logic Function

Step 2: Identify the Question Type

The question asks for the *purpose* of something mentioned in the passage, making this a Logic Function question.

Step 3: Research the Relevant Text

The question directly points to lines 6–8, but be sure to consider that line's context within the paragraph as a whole.

Step 4: Make a Prediction

The first paragraph focuses mostly on the theory of utilitarianism. While the author (and Rawls) ultimately complain about utilitarianism, the question being asked about (essentially, why not try to maximize satisfaction?) shows how, "[a]t first sight, utilitarianism seems plausible." In other words, it points to a reason why people would have accepted utilitarianism in the first place.

Step 5: Evaluate the Answer Choices

(D) matches the idea of showing something plausible about utilitarianism.

(A) is a 180. The question illustrates why utilitarianism *does* seem plausible at first. Problems with utilitarianism are not brought up until later in the paragraph.

(B) is a Distortion. Utilitarianism is never described as "internally contradictory." In addition, the question shows off why utilitarianism is *plausible*, not problematic.

(C) is Extreme. The question merely illustrates why utilitarianism is *plausible*, not why it "must be true."

(E) is a Distortion. The question being posed describes the basic tenet of utilitarianism. It does not offer any way of *supplementing* that theory.

3. (B) Global

Step 2: Identify the Question Type

The question asks for the primary purpose of the whole passage. Any question that asks about the passage in its entirety is a Global question.

Step 3: Research the Relevant Text

As with any Global question, the entire text is relevant. Instead of going back to the text, just consider the overall Purpose as predicted when reading the passage.

Step 4: Make a Prediction

While the author offers the occasional opinion, the bulk of the passage is focused on merely describing Rawls's theory as an alternative to the flawed theory of utilitarianism.

Step 5: Evaluate the Answer Choices

(B) is correct, focusing on Rawls's theory as a reaction toward the problematic theory of utilitarianism.

(A) is too narrow. Reasons for abandoning utilitarianism are raised in the first paragraph, but this ignores the focus of the rest of the passage, which is all about Rawls's theory.

(C) is problematic for a couple of reasons. First, no information is given about the "historical development" of Rawls's theory. Further, that theory is never described as *celebrated*.

(D) is a Distortion. While the author offers the occasional opinion on Rawls's theory, the bulk of the passage is not concerned with *debating* the pros and cons. Further, it's never suggested that the theory is *complex*.

(E) is a 180, at worst. The theory is never said to be *controversial*. Further, the author brings up reservations at the end of the passage, which hardly suggests that there's concrete truth to the theory.

4. (A) Inference

Step 2: Identify the Question Type

The question asks for something with which Rawls and the author are "mostly likely to agree," making this an Inference question.

Step 3: Research the Relevant Text

Both Rawls and the author provide opinions throughout the passage, so the entire text is relevant.

Step 4: Make a Prediction

The question is too open-ended to make a specific prediction. Stick to the big picture (the veil of ignorance theory is clever, albeit flawed), and test the answers one at a time.

Step 5: Evaluate the Answer Choices

(A) is supported. Both the author and Rawls reject utilitarianism, which is about fulfilling the majority's preferences (lines 4–5). The author-approved part of Rawls's theory allows for solutions made by "individuals motivated by self-interest" (lines 40–42).

(B) is a 180. Rawls's theory is based on people motivated by self-interest, not people who set aside that self-interest.

(C) is a 180. This is the redistributionist idea raised at the very end of the passage (lines 53–55). The author's use of the word [*u*]*nfortunately* (line 51) indicates disapproval of the concept, rather than agreement.

(D) is a Distortion. In the discussion of primary goods in the last paragraph, there is no mention of what "most people" believe or what anyone would consider to be "most valuable."

(E) is a 180. Maximizing the satisfaction of the majority is a tenet of utilitarianism, the theory that both Rawls and the author reject.

5. (E) Inference

Step 2: Identify the Question Type

The question asks for the author's stance toward Rawls's theory. The author never directly asserts a stance, but the stance can be deduced by analyzing the author's language, making this an Inference question.

Step 3: Research the Relevant Text

The author's reaction to Rawls is scattered throughout the passage, notably via the Keywords *ingenious* (line 19), *clever* (line 26), and [*u*]*nfortunately* (line 51).

Step 4: Make a Prediction

The words *ingenious* and *clever* indicate that the author appreciates Rawls's theory to some extent. However, the word [*u*]*nfortunately* suggests that the author is ultimately not convinced. The original problem (some people will lose out) still exists.

Step 5: Evaluate the Answer Choices

(E) matches the author's tone, both in the clear admiration for some ideas and in the ultimate disappointment in the theory's shortcoming.

(A) is a 180. The author clearly has opinions that belie any "scholarly neutrality."

(B) is Extreme. The author may see the ultimate result as unfortunate, but that hardly qualifies as *disdain*. Furthermore, if there's any disappointment, it has nothing to do with any pretensions.

(C) is a Distortion. The author never exactly questions the theory's cogency (i.e., its effectiveness). The author merely questions whether the theory is really the right solution to the problem of utilitarianism.

(D) is Extreme. The author is impressed with the ideas, but the unfortunate end effect suggests that the author isn't entirely enthusiastic.

6. (C) Logic Reasoning (Weaken)

Step 2: Identify the Question Type

The question asks for something that would "call into question" a claim in the passage. This is the same kind of language used for Weaken questions in the Logical Reasoning section.

Step 3: Research the Relevant Text

The question is directed at the claim in lines 49–51, but use the surrounding lines for context.

Step 4: Make a Prediction

This claim in question is all part of Rawls's theory. An "individual in the original position" refers back to the fourth paragraph, which describes people motivated by self-interest but ignorant of their standing. Self-interest will lead to solutions in which individuals "will not lose, because nobody loses" (line 42). That supports the claim in question, which suggests that individuals will act so that "everyone should get at least a minimum." To weaken that idea, the correct answer will show this won't always happen—sometimes people will act in a way that leads to somebody getting nothing.

Step 5: Evaluate the Answer Choices

(C) weakens the claim. If some people are willing to risk "a complete loss," then that means they're taking a chance that somebody will get nothing, as opposed to ensuring everyone gets a minimum.

(A) does not weaken the claim. Under Rawls's theory, people can still be motivated by self-interest and put their preferences over those of others—as long as everybody gets at least *something*.

(B) is irrelevant. While this may deny the potential for Rawls's theory to work in practice (as nobody could be in the "original position"), it does not affect the *theoretical* idea that such people would agree on giving everyone a bare minimum.

(D) is irrelevant. Rawls's theory is not about guaranteeing satisfaction. It's about doing what's fair and just.

(E) is irrelevant. The availability of resources has no effect on whether people would believe in the concept of giving everyone a minimum of primary goods.

Passage 2: The Great Migration

Step 1: Read the Passage Strategically

Sample Roadmap

line #	Keyword/phrase	¶ Margin notes
4	While	Great migration
8	three catalysts; First	3 catalysts
10	Second	
13	Finally	
16	because; only then	Cause: income gap
19	Less clear; however	Why continued?
23	propose	Auth: momentum made it easier
26	typically assumed	Migrate if earnings > difficulties
30	suggests	3 difficulties
31	First	
34	Second	
36	Third	
41	show	Studies:
45	Thus	How migrating made easier
51	Additionally	

Discussion

The opening note indicates this passage was written by three people. Thankfully, there is no need to juggle multiple points of view. The passage is written in one voice, and the note is merely for grammatical purposes (e.g., to explain the use of *we* in line 23 and to accurately refer to plural *authors* in the question stems).

The first paragraph introduces the **Topic**: The Great Migration of African Americans in the United States from the South to the North. The authors provide three causes of this event: 1) Employers in the North needed more workers. 2) With fewer immigrants coming in, those employers turned to the South more for laborers. 3) Work in the South was dwindling as crop problems arose.

The second paragraph neatly sums it up: the migration was caused by a significant income gap. People in the South needed jobs, and the North needed workers. *However*, the authors then raise a significant question: why did migration continue for decades even after the income gap decreased? This question serves as the **Scope** of the passage.

The authors provide an answer in the third paragraph. Once the migration started, it created momentum that made it easier for others to migrate. The rest of the passage simply presents detailed support for this idea. First, the third paragraph outlines three difficulties that would have hindered migration: 1) a lack of information about housing and employment opportunities available; 2) the cost, in terms of time and money, of moving; and 3) the need to adapt to a new environment.

The last paragraph provides data showing how the Great Migration overcame each of those difficulties: 1) People in the South learned about opportunities through letters and conversations with original migrants who came back to visit. 2) Later migrants saved on costs by basically hitching a ride with earlier migrants returning North after a visit to the South. 3) Early migrants helped newer migrants adjust to the new environment.

The **Purpose** of the passage was to describe factors involved in the Great Migration. The **Main Idea** is that the Great Migration was initially caused by an income gap, while other factors gave the migration momentum to continue for decades afterward.

7. (E) Global

Step 2: Identify the Question Type

The question asks for the "main point of the passage." As it asks about the passage in its entirety, this is a Global question.

Step 3: Research the Relevant Text

As with any Global question, the entire text is relevant. Instead of going back into the text, use the Main Idea predicted after reading the passage.

Step 4: Make a Prediction

The passage is focused entirely on what caused the Great Migration to start and what helped it continue. While income gap was the initial cause, the authors claim that other factors reduced the difficulty of migration, helping the Great Migration continue for decades afterward.

Step 5: Evaluate the Answer Choices

(E) is correct, providing a vague (although accurate) summary of the Great Migration's initial cause and why it continued for so long.

(A) is merely a detail from the first paragraph. This misses the passage's focus on *why* this event occurred.

(B) accurately cites some of the initial causes outlined in the first paragraph, but completely omits the last three paragraphs that focus on why the migration persisted after the initial trigger.

(C) is too narrow. This highlights one of the reasons listed in the last paragraph for the extended duration of the Great Migration. However, that's just one point among many. The main point of the passage and the main reason for the continued migration involves much more than just financial costs.

(D) is a Distortion. This takes details that apply to the Great Migration and applies them to migrations in general. The authors never suggest this is true of migrations in general, and that certainly wasn't the point of the passage.

8. (A) Detail

Step 2: Identify the Question Type

The phrase "[a]ccording to the passage" suggests the answer to the question will be mentioned directly in the text. That makes this a Detail question.

Step 3: Research the Relevant Text

The authors explain why the Great Migration did not start earlier than 1915 in lines 16–19 ("began in 1915 and not earlier").

Step 4: Make a Prediction

In lines 16–19, the authors directly explain why the Great Migration did not start before 1915: "it was only then that the North-South income gap became large enough to start such a large-scale migration."

Step 5: Evaluate the Answer Choices

(A) is an exact paraphrase of the authors' claim.

(B) is Extreme. There may have been a gap in income, but that's not to say the cost of living in the North was "prohibitively high." The authors never state or suggest that this was an issue.

(C) brings up the need for specialized training, a concept that is never mentioned in the passage.

(D) is a Distortion. While momentum made it easier for later migrants to move, the authors never claim that a *lack* of momentum was what prevented migration to start in the first place.

(E) is not mentioned in the passage. The boll weevil infestation led to reduced labor demand (lines 13–15), but there's no suggestion that agricultural jobs paid "very well" before that happened.

9. (D) Logic Function

Step 2: Identify the Question Type

The question asks how two paragraphs *function*, making this easy to identify as a Logic Function question.

Step 3: Research the Relevant Text

Instead of going back into the specific text, use margin notes and focus on how the third and fourth paragraphs relate to the earlier paragraphs and the passage as a whole.

Step 4: Make a Prediction

The third and fourth paragraph outline difficulties that hinder migration and how the Great Migration overcame those difficulties. This is all part of what the authors *propose* (line 23) as a response to the question of "why migration continued"—a concept raised in the second paragraph (lines 19–21).

Step 5: Evaluate the Answer Choices

(D) correctly describes how the last two paragraphs help answer the question posed in the second paragraph.

(A) is a Distortion. The explanation in the first paragraph outlines why the Great Migration started in the first place. The third and fourth paragraphs do nothing to change that. Instead, they provide an explanation why the Great Migration *continued* afterward.

(B) mentions repercussions of the Great Migration, which are never addressed. The passage is focused merely on why it happened, not what resulted from it.

(C) is a Distortion. The last two paragraphs do not present a historical model, nor do they utilize any evidence from the first two paragraphs.

(E) is a Distortion. The claims in the first paragraph are about the initial cause of the Great Migration. The claims in the third and fourth paragraphs are completely separate and explain

why the migration continued afterward. There is no additional support for the initial cause.

10. (A) Inference

Step 2: Identify the Question Type

The correct answer will be something with which the authors are "most likely to agree." It will not be directly stated but will be fully supported by information in the passage, making this an Inference question.

Step 3: Research the Relevant Text

There are no line references or content clues, so the entire text is relevant.

Step 4: Make a Prediction

It's difficult to predict an answer here; there are too many possible inferences. Instead, eliminate answers that are clearly beyond the Scope of the passage, and use content clues in the answer choices to do any necessary research.

Step 5: Evaluate the Answer Choices

(A) is supported starting in lines 25–29 and continuing throughout the rest of the passage. The likelihood of migration is not determined by expected financial gains alone. One also needs to consider potential difficulties such as uncertain prospects, travel costs, the need for cultural adjustment, and more.

(B) is Extreme. The authors never mention what triggered "nineteenth-century migrations" (i.e., ones from the 1800s), so there is no suggestion that explaining the Great Migration *must* begin with such accounts.

(C) is not supported. The authors only focus on the Great Migration and never compare it to other migrations.

(D) is Extreme. The authors only focus on the Great Migration. There is no indication of what's true for *most* large-scale migrations, let alone any migration other than the one described.

(E) is not supported. In fact, the authors suggest there were migrations as early as the nineteenth century (lines 4–6). There's no indication whether these were or not, but there's also no suggestion that there weren't large-scale migrations elsewhere in the world at any other time before the twentieth century.

11. (D) Logic Function

Step 2: Identify the Question Type

The question asks for the *purpose* of one sentence, making this a Logic Function question.

Step 3: Research the Relevant Text

The question directly asks about the last sentence of the second paragraph (lines 19–22), but be sure to consider its context within the whole paragraph as well as within the passage as a whole.

Step 4: Make a Prediction

The sentence in question mentions how the Great Migration continued for decades after it started, even though the income gap got smaller. This raises the very question that is answered by what the authors *propose* in the third and fourth paragraphs. It is essentially the setup for everything the authors discuss in the rest of the passage.

Step 5: Evaluate the Answer Choices

(D) correctly identifies the sentence as what the authors explain throughout the remainder of the passage.

(A) is a Distortion. While earlier research may have left the claim in question unexplained, there is no suggestion that earlier research was *misguided*.

(B) is a Distortion. The initial causes of the Great Migration are not extended to any other event. Further, the continued migration is based on entirely new explanations described later in the passage.

(C) is a 180. The claim in question states the income differences were narrowing after 1915, which actually suggests that the income in the North *was* indeed higher beforehand.

(E) is Extreme and a 180. It is "[l]ess clear," but that doesn't mean it *cannot* be explained. In fact, the entire second half of the passage provides an explanation.

12. (C) Inference

Step 2: Identify the Question Type

The correct answer will be a statement supported by passage, making this an Inference question.

Step 3: Research the Relevant Text

There are no line references or content clues, so the entire text is relevant.

Step 4: Make a Prediction

The correct answer could be based on anything from the passage, so it's not possible to make a solid prediction. Eliminate answers that are clearly beyond the Scope of the passage, and use content clues in the answers to do any necessary research.

Step 5: Evaluate the Answer Choices

(C) is supported. The increased labor demand in the North and the decreased labor demand in the South are mentioned in lines 8–15 as catalysts for the Great Migration. The phrase "[i]n short" in the following paragraph suggests that all of the details from lines 8–15 led to a simplistic causal factor: the income gap.

(A) is a Distortion. There may have been an overall gap in income, but there's no way of comparing individual jobs within distinct industries.

(B) is not supported. There is no indication that earlier migrants had more jobs to choose from.

(D) is not supported. The 1910s and the 1920s were when labor demand decreased in the South (lines 13–15), but there's no suggestion that wages remained constant for all workers during that time. In fact, wages are never mentioned.

(E) is Extreme. The studies in the last paragraph definitely indicate migrants returning to the South and bringing back information, but there's no indication that *most* migrants did so.

13. (B) Logic Reasoning (Strengthen)

Step 2: Identify the Question Type

The question asks for something that "would provide the most support" for the authors' analysis, making this a Strengthen question like those found in Logical Reasoning.

Step 3: Research the Relevant Text

The authors' primary conclusion starts off the third paragraph and is supported by all of the subsequent details.

Step 4: Make a Prediction

The authors are primarily focused on why the migration persisted for so long. Their proposal is that momentum made it easier for people to migrate (lines 23–25). The evidence is that many of the difficulties described in paragraph 3 were addressed by the solutions listed in paragraph 4. To further support the authors' proposal, the correct answer will merely provide further evidence that migration was made easier and that difficulties were overcome.

Step 5: Evaluate the Answer Choices

(B) supports the authors' proposal. One of the difficulties migrants faced was having to "adapt to a new culture or language" (lines 39–40). This was addressed in the last line, as early migrants provided a "cultural cushion for later migrants, so that they did not have to struggle as hard." If these migrants moved into communities with people of common origins, that would certainly help provide a "cultural cushion" to reduce the shock of entering a whole new area.

(A) is a 180. This suggests it took longer to find jobs as time went on, which would make things harder, not easier.

(C) is a 180. Fluctuations would cause uncertainty, which would be harder to deal with than constant prices.

(D) is irrelevant. This puts more pressure on Northern employers, but does nothing to explain why people from the South were more likely to migrate. Even if there were more people recruiting in the South, that doesn't mean migrating was any easier.

(E) is irrelevant. What happened after the Great Migration does nothing to support why people moved up North in the first place.

Passage 3: Insider Trading

Step 1: Read the Passage Strategically

Sample Roadmap

line #	Keyword/phrase	¶ Margin notes
Passage A		
–	–	Insider trading law
6	However	Auth: shouldn't be a crime
8	?	
16	best	Market works best when all info available
21	helps	stock prices reflect info
26	helps	Selling stock provides more accurate info
27	help ensure	
29	good	
31-32	helps to consider	Nontrading also happens
34	but	not a problem
35	rightfully	
36	No one	
Passage B		
37	basic principles	Stock market transparent
41	only	success by analysis of info
50	unfairly compromises	insider trading based on unshared info
51	:	Auth: unfair
53	difficult or impossible	
55	causes	Consequences: investors lose confidence
56	could ultimately destroy	leads to widespread problems
58	whole point	
62	thus	
63–64	could ultimately lead to	

Discussion

Passage A immediately introduces the **Topic**: insider trading, which involves making stock transactions based on information that hasn't been made public. The first paragraph states that this a crime; *however*, the author suggests in the second paragraph that it shouldn't be. The author instead raises the idea that insider trading actually aligns perfectly with the model of a properly functioning stock market. This question of whether insider trading is criminal serves as the **Scope** of the passage.

The author then describes how the stock market functions in general, in a way that parallels insider trading. Stock brokers analyze data and gain information that others don't have. They then use this knowledge to buy and sell. Nothing criminal. It's just the way the system works. The next couple of paragraphs continue this theme by further describing an effective stock market, again as a thinly veiled comparison to insider trading. Stock markets work best when everyone has access to all relevant information, and that information is reflected in the stock prices. So, if someone knows the value of a stock will drop and acts on that information, that sends a signal to others who can then better assess the stock's value. Everyone wins!

In the final paragraph, the author provides one final point in favor of insider trading. There's a similar, more common practice called "insider nontrading." This also involves making decisions based on inside information, but it results in people *not* buying or selling—and yet nobody seems to have a problem with that. In the end, the **Purpose** of the passage is to argue in favor of insider trading. The **Main Idea** is that insider trading should not be a crime because it is beneficial and works exactly the way the stock market is supposed to.

Passage B also talks about the stock market (**Topic**). The first paragraph describes the significance of transparency: making sure everyone has access to the same information to make good investing decisions. This leads to the second paragraph, which begins a discussion of insider trading and why it's bad for the stock market (**Scope**). When people act on information that others don't have, they are getting an unfair advantage that makes it difficult for others to make money.

This leads to severe consequences described in the third paragraph. When it's difficult to make money, investors lose confidence in the market. They then stop investing, which means companies lose funding, which ultimately can lead to "widespread financial repercussions." By the end, it's clear the **Purpose** of passage B is to argue against insider trading, with the **Main Idea** that insider trading gives some people an unfair advantage that, over time, can lead to financial disaster.

Both passages focus on how insider trading affects the stock market. The author of passage A sees insider trading as a benefit, while the author of passage B sees it as a problem. Despite the clear discrepancy, a lot of their arguments are based on shared common principles (e.g., open access to information and analyzing that information is crucial to success in the stock market). However, there are a few notable differences. Only passage A brings up the legality of insider trading, and only passage B goes beyond insider trading to discuss investor confidence and financial impact on companies.

14. (D) Global

Step 2: Identify the Question Type

The question asks for the "primary concern" of both passages as a whole, making this a Global question.

Step 3: Research the Relevant Text

As with all Global questions, the entire text is relevant. Use the Purpose and Main Idea of each passage, as predicted while reading the passages.

Step 4: Make a Prediction

Both passages are focused on whether insider trading is good for the stock market or not. The correct answer will raise the question of its impact on the stock market.

Step 5: Evaluate the Answer Choices

(D) correctly raises a question about each passage's central purpose. Passage A argues that insider trading is not harmful, while passage B argues that it is.

(A) is too narrow. Both passages do define insider trading, but only at one point for the sake of clarity. Both passages spend far more time discussing the benefits and problems with insider trading.

(B) brings up penalties for insider trading, a concept not addressed by either author.

(C) is a Distortion. Both authors focus on the *effect* of insider trading, not on the motive for doing so in the first place.

(E) mentions regulating insider training, a concept that neither author addresses.

15. (B) Inference

Step 2: Identify the Question Type

The question asks about the authors' attitudes. Attitudes are not stated directly but can be deduced based on the tone of each passage. This is a common variant of an Inference question.

Step 3: Research the Relevant Text

Insider trading is discussed throughout both passages, so there is a lot of relevant text. Use the big picture and Keywords to get a sense of the attitudes.

Step 4: Make a Prediction

The Main Idea of passage A is that insider trading is actually beneficial, as evidenced by the line "good for everyone" (line 29). The Main Idea of passage B is that insider trading is a problem, as evidenced by the line "unfairly compromises the market" (lines 50–51). The correct answer will express, in order, passage A's positive stance and B's negative stance.

Step 5: Evaluate the Answer Choices

(B) correctly identifies passage A's author as positive and passage B's author as negative.

(A) correctly identifies the author of passage A as positive. However, the author of passage B claims insider trading is unfair, which is hardly a neutral assessment.

(C) suggests that the author of passage A is neutral, but that author ultimately suggests that the concept of insider training is "good for everyone"—a decisively non-neutral claim.

(D) suggests that both authors are neutral. However, the author of passage A suggests that insider trading is good, and the author of passage B says it's unfair. These are not neutral claims.

(E) suggests the author of passage A is negative, which is a 180 from that author's suggestion that insider trading is "good for everyone."

16. (C) Inference

Step 2: Identify the Question Type

The question asks for something with which both authors are "most likely to agree." The correct answer will not be stated, but will be directly supported by information in the passages, making this an Inference question.

Step 3: Research the Relevant Text

There are no line references or content clues, so all of the text is relevant.

Step 4: Make a Prediction

While vague Inference questions are often difficult, if not impossible, to predict, the relationship between these passages provides some helpful information. The authors are mostly in disagreement, making it a little easier to spot points of *agreement*. Sure enough, both authors base their arguments on two general principles. First, it's important that relevant information be openly available (lines 16–18 and lines 37–40). Second, success in the market depends on analyzing the information effectively (lines 8–15 and lines

40–42). The correct answer will likely match up with at least one of these principles.

Step 5: Evaluate the Answer Choices

(C) is consistent with both authors' arguments. The author of passage A claims that analyzing stock to take advantage is part of the job (lines 8–15), and the author of passage B claims that success depends on using analysis to get an advantage (lines 40–42).

(A) is a major point of the last paragraph of passage B, but the author of passage A presents no opinion on how insider trading impacts investor confidence.

(B) is Extreme. The author of passage A says all *relevant* information (lines 16–17) should be available, and the author of passage B only mentions information "that influences trading decisions." Neither of those phrases are enough to suggest that *all* information should be available—only information relevant to the stock market.

(D) brings up insider nontrading, which only passage A mentions. The author of passage B presents no opinion on that concept.

(E) is Extreme and likely a 180. While the author of passage A is in favor of insider trading, there is no suggestion that it offers the *best* means for spreading information. Besides, the author of passage B finds insider trading to be unfair and would certainly disagree with this claim.

17. (E) Inference

Step 2: Identify the Question Type

The question asks for a law that would conform to an author's position. That can sound very much like a Principle question in Logical Reasoning. However, passage A brings up insider trading laws, so the correct answer will not be any more general than the information provided. It will merely be supported by the information provided in the passage, making this an Inference question. Regardless of what you call it, there will be direct logical support for the correct answer.

Step 3: Research the Relevant Text

The question asks about something that conforms to a general position, which is part of the big picture. There is no specific line or paragraph to research. The entire text is relevant.

Step 4: Make a Prediction

The author of passage A is firmly in favor of insider trading, while the author of passage B is firmly against it. The correct answer will be a law that makes it acceptable to make transactions based on inside information, thus conforming to passage A and *not* passage B.

Step 5: Evaluate the Answer Choices

(E) is consistent with the position stated in passage A. As long as the information is legitimately acquired, the author of passage A finds insider trading perfectly acceptable.

(A) is a 180. The author of passage A approves of insider trading as it would "help ensure that stock prices do reflect a more accurate assessment of all the relevant facts" (lines 27–29).

(B) is a 180. The author of passage A accepts trading based on all relevant information, regardless of whether it's publicly known or learned from the inside.

(C) is a 180. The author of passage A has no opinion on the effect on investor confidence. Furthermore, this is the kind of law the author of passage B would endorse, which is the opposite of what's being asked.

(D) is not supported. The author of passage A is fine with insider trading regardless of the transaction type. There is no suggestion that selling is okay but not buying.

18. (B) Logic Reasoning (Method of Argument)

Step 2: Identify the Question Type

The word *by* indicates that the question is asking *how* the author of passage A argues, as opposed to *what* the argument says. That's the sign of a Method of Argument question like the ones found in Logical Reasoning.

Step 3: Research the Relevant Text

Methods are not derived from any one line or paragraph in particular, so the entire text is relevant here. Focus on the big picture and the overall structure of the passage.

Step 4: Make a Prediction

The correct answer has to include something the author of passage A does but not something the author of passage B does. While passage B discusses insider trading and its potential effects, passage A makes comparisons of insider trading to permissible activities. The bulk of the passage describes the stock market in general and why it's important to have information spread widely and quickly. The passage concludes with a discussion of a "widespread practice." Because insider nontrading is permissible, the author of passage A feels insider trading should be as well. The correct answer will point out this analogical approach.

Step 5: Evaluate the Answer Choices

(B) is correct, as it describes the method used by passage A, comparing a controversial activity (insider trading) with more acceptable ones (general stock market activities and insider nontrading). In lines 14–15, the author of passage A says that researching and taking advantage of knowledge that others might not means "you've done your homework." In line 36,

the author of passage A emphasizes that "[n]o one" would think to criminalize insider nontrading.

(A) mentions application of principles to "particular examples." Neither author offers any specific examples of insider trading.

(C) is a 180. Passage B describes consequences in the final paragraph, so this is *not* a method that is unlike the one used in passage B.

(D) is a 180. This is not unlike passage B. Passage B directly relates the effect of insider trading to a large context in the last paragraph.

(E) brings up the motivation behind insider trading, a concept that is never addressed in either passage.

19. (D) Logic Function

Step 2: Identify the Question Type

The question asks how two references relate to one another. It's difficult to characterize this question by the stem alone. However, a glance at the answers reveals that each answer lists the purpose each reference serves within the passages, making this a Logic Function question.

Step 3: Research the Relevant Text

The question stem provides line references, but be sure to consider how those lines fit within the context of the paragraphs in which they appear as well as the passages as a whole.

Step 4: Make a Prediction

The author of passage A discusses analysis of stock information in the second paragraph, which is meant to show how insider trading is actually consistent with such analysis, and is thus not really a criminal act. The author of passage B discusses analysis as part of a transparent market, which is undermined by insider trading as described in the second paragraph. In essence, both authors bring up analysis to support conflicting opinions about insider trading. The correct answer will be consistent with that dichotomy.

Step 5: Evaluate the Answer Choices

(D) matches the opposing purposes of each reference.

(A) accurately fits the tone of passage B. However, passage A points to analysis as part of how a stock market is supposed to work. It's definitely not *unnecessary*.

(B) is a Distortion. The author of passage A never suggests that there's a "lack of transparency" in the stock market.

(C) is a Distortion on both parts. The author of passage A never suggests that anything is unfair—only the author of passage B does that. And passage B suggests that transparency makes analysis possible, not the other way around.

(E) is Extreme. The author of passage A never suggests that stock analysis is limited solely to brokers and stock-market professionals.

Passage 4: Brain Scans

Step 1: Read the Passage Strategically

Sample Roadmap

line #	Keyword/phrase	¶ Margin notes
1	problems	Brain scans: OK for medical
4	for example	problem w/ psych
6	value	Assumption: brain is modular
7	indubitable; However	
8	fundamentally	
9	different	
10	depends on a premise	
15	may in fact	Uttal: brain activity general, not modular
18	contends; rather than	
19	likely	
21	cannot be said	
22	for instance	
28	But; if; critique	Why do brain scans "light up"?
29	valid	fMRI -- measures oxygen levels
30	in fact	subtractive method
31	?	
37	But; actually	
38	:	
43	seemingly plausible	
47	immediately obvious	Problem w/ subtractive method --
48	problem; obscures	whole brain active
50	false impression	
53	striking	
54	But; ultimately	
55	attractive; because	
56	?	

Discussion

The opening sentence introduces the **Topic** (brain scans) and the **Scope** (problems with their use for measuring mental activity). The author accepts brain scans for medical uses (e.g., discovering a brain tumor). *However*, the author is less convinced about psychological applications. The author claims that psychological use of brain scans rests on the assumption that the brain is made up of independent modules.

This modular theory is disputed in the second paragraph by psychologist William Uttal. According to Uttal, mental processes are not entirely independent and are part of general brain activity. This is illustrated by the example of emotion and reasoning. The author argues that these mental processes can't necessarily be separated, as some would suggest otherwise.

In the third paragraph, the author brings up a paradox. If mental activities are not modular, why do certain areas of the brain "light up" when people perform certain tasks? As an example, the author describes an fMRI. An fMRI is meant to show how much oxygen is used in different areas of the brain at any given time. *But* the author suggests that that's not quite accurate. It actually shows a *difference*. It starts with an initial measurement of oxygen usage. When a task is being performed, the fMRI subtracts that initial value. Anything above normal is said to apply solely to the given task.

In the last paragraph, the author cites the problem with this method: it gives a false impression. Some parts of the brain might be working more, but the whole brain is still working. The subtractive method (as the author calls it) only shows what's working in excess. It fails to show the rest of the brain that may also be working on the task. So, the **Purpose** of the passage is to provide evidence against using brain scans for psychological purposes. The **Main Idea** is that brain scans are not good for psychological purposes because the brain is not necessarily modular, as assumed, and the results don't necessarily provide an accurate picture of what's really happening throughout the entire brain.

20. (B) Global

Step 2: Identify the Question Type

The question asks for the "main point of the passage" as a whole, making this a Global question.

Step 3: Research the Relevant Text

As with all Global questions, the entire text is relevant. Focus on the big picture and use the Main Idea as predicted when reading the passage.

Step 4: Make a Prediction

Ultimately, the author is arguing that brain scans are not good for psychological purposes. Using them relies on a bad

assumption (the brain is modular) and the results don't show everything that's happening in the brain.

Step 5: Evaluate the Answer Choices

(B) matches the author's concerns about using brain scans for psychological purposes (to depict mental activity).

(A) is a Distortion. The author mentions "widespread use of brain scans" (line 2), but never says anything about their usage growing *rapidly*. Besides, this puts too much emphasis on their increased usage and makes the true focus of the passage (the problems) a mere side note.

(C) is a Distortion and far too specific. This merely takes one detail from the second paragraph (lines 21–24) and twists the meaning. Even if this were accurate, it hardly expresses the point of the passage as a whole. It completely ignores everything else in the surrounding paragraphs.

(D) is Extreme and too narrow. This focuses too much on the fMRI problem and ignores the entire first two paragraphs about the modular theory. Besides, the author says the results of fMRI provide a "false impression." That doesn't mean the results are *false*. The results are accurate; they just don't provide a complete picture.

(E) is too narrow, concentrating on the rhetorical question at the end. Sure, the author suggests that the subtractive method makes the modular theory look attractive. However, the author never suggests that's the *precise* reason for its widespread currency. Besides, this completely ignores the rest of the passage that focuses on the problem with the modular theory and the subtractive method.

21. (A) Detail

Step 2: Identify the Question Type

The question asks for a fact about mental activity as it was "described in the passage." That makes this a Detail question.

Step 3: Research the Relevant Text

The correct answer will be based directly on what was stated about the modular theory, which is described in the first paragraph.

Step 4: Make a Prediction

The term "modular theory" is mentioned in line 14 and refers to the premise outlined in lines 10–13. It states that "the mind [and thus mental activity] can be analyzed into separate and distinct modules" that are "instantiated in localized regions of the brain."

Step 5: Evaluate the Answer Choices

(A) matches the text precisely.

(B) is a Distortion, if not a 180. Metabolic activity is mentioned in the third paragraph, separate from any discussion of the modular theory. Further, the modular theory suggests that any given mental activity is limited to a single distinct region of the brain. It would not suggest activity is required "in *all* parts of the brain."

(C) is unsupported. It is said that mental activity consists of physical processes (lines 15–16), but there is no indication that people have "limited control" over them.

(D) is a Faulty Use of Detail. There are certain mental activities (emotion and reasoning) that are said to be localized to these areas (lines 22–23), but that doesn't mean all mental activity in general is localized in those areas.

(E) is a 180. Reason-giving is just one mental process that is said to be localized in the prefrontal cortex (line 23). However, the modular theory considers that separate from other mental processes. So other mental activity would be *distinct* from reason-giving.

22. (D) Inference

Step 2: Identify the Question Type

The question asks for something with which the author is "most likely to agree." Therefore, the correct answer won't be stated directly, but it will be a valid inference based on the passage.

Step 3: Research the Relevant Text

The question asks about the subtractive method, which the author describes in the third paragraph and evaluates in the fourth paragraph.

Step 4: Make a Prediction

Because the question is asking about the author's opinion, the correct answer is more likely to come from the opinions presented in the fourth paragraph rather than the factual description in the third. The author argues that the subtractive method *obscures* (line 48) certain facts and provides a "false impression" (line 50). The author clearly has a problem with the method, but does suggest that the "striking images" created by it are what make it seem attractive (lines 52–56). The correct answer will be consistent with these opinions.

Step 5: Evaluate the Answer Choices

(D) is supported. While the author clearly sees the problem with the subtractive method, it does provide images that make the modular theory *attractive* (line 55).

(A) is perfect...until the last two words. The author's argument is that the results are problematic for *psychological* applications, not medical applications. The author fully accepts using brain scans for medical purposes (lines 3–7).

(B) is a 180. The subtractive method actually "obscures the fact that the entire brain is active" (lines 48–49).

(C) is not supported and likely a 180. It's actually likely that the images *do* show a lot of activity in the amygdala when someone experiences anger. However, the author's point is that the *rest* of the brain is *also* active, even if that doesn't show up when the subtractive method is used.

(E) is a 180. The subtractive method *does* depict differential rates of oxygen use (lines 37–38). Any misconception is based on how people *interpret* that data, not on recognizing how that information is measured.

23. (E) Logic Function

Step 2: Identify the Question Type

The question asks for the "central function" of a paragraph, making this a Logic Function question.

Step 3: Research the Relevant Text

Be sure to consult the margin notes for the final paragraph, and consider how it relates to all of the preceding paragraphs.

Step 4: Make a Prediction

Start by considering the author's main purpose: the author is rejecting the modular theory. That rejection happens in the second paragraph. The modular theory is supposedly backed up by the subtractive method, as described in the third paragraph. However, the purpose of the final paragraph (which this question is asking about) is to dispute the method described in the third paragraph, thus reinforcing the author's argument in the second paragraph.

Step 5: Evaluate the Answer Choices

(E) accurately matches the author's intention. The final paragraph disputes the evidence in the third paragraph (about the subtractive method) to further the author's case that the modular theory is flawed—the point raised in the second paragraph.

(A) begins well, stating that the last paragraph criticizes the results described in the third paragraph. However, those results are *not* incompatible with the premise from the first paragraph (the modular theory). In fact, the author admits in the last sentence that the results *do* illustrate the modular theory well.

(B) is a 180. The author disputes the modular theory (the position from the first paragraph). The author never calls for that theory to be modified. Besides, the author admits in the last sentence that the results from the third paragraph actually work well with the modular theory. They would support the theory, not be a basis for modifying the theory.

(C) is a Distortion. The author never suggests any model (let alone the basis for the research in the third paragraph) is *outdated*.

(D) is a Distortion. The author does argue that the method described in the third paragraph is deceptive and thus inadequate for supporting the view in the first paragraph. However, the author never disputes the argument in the second paragraph or calls it inadequate. After all, the second paragraph contains the author's own argument.

24. (A) Logic Function

Step 2: Identify the Question Type

The phrase "in order to" indicates that the question is asking *why* the author draws an analogy, which makes this a Logic Function question.

Step 3: Research the Relevant Text

The analogy between brain scans and X-rays is made in line 5. Be sure to consider the surrounding lines for context.

Step 4: Make a Prediction

In comparing brain scans to X-rays, the author is showing how, "As applied to medical diagnosis," the value of brain scans is "straightforward and indubitable" (lines 3–7). That analogy is followed swiftly by a [*h*]*owever*, which sets up the contrasting view that brain scans are not as clearly applicable to psychology. So, the purpose of the analogy is to show how brain scans can be useful in one area, despite being inapplicable in another.

Step 5: Evaluate the Answer Choices

(A) accurately expresses the author's intention. The analogy describes a valid use for brain scans, which contrasts the rest of the passage that shows their use in psychology is not necessarily as valuable.

(B) is not supported. The author is not concerned with "new technology."

(C) is a 180 at worst. The author claims a brain scan and an X-ray are *similar*. There is no suggestion that one is any less precise than the other.

(D) is a Distortion. X-rays are not used by the author to undermine any theory. The modular theory is disputed later based on entirely different evidence.

(E) is a Distortion. Brain scans and X-rays are said to be similar, but it's never suggested that one *evolved* from the other.

25. (E) Detail

Step 2: Identify the Question Type

The phrase "[a]ccording to the passage" indicates that the correct answer will be directly stated in the passage, making this a Detail question.

Step 3: Research the Relevant Text

The question asks about William Uttal, whose ideas are presented in the second paragraph.

Step 4: Make a Prediction

The question refers directly to lines 18–21, which state that Uttal contends that mental processes are "properties of a more general mental activity that is distributed throughout the brain."

Step 5: Evaluate the Answer Choices

(E) matches the text of the passage nearly word for word.

(A) is a 180. Uttal argues that mental processes are *not* distinct and cannot be decomposed into individual modules.

(B) is a Distortion. The author suggests that it's absurd to "cleanly separate emotion from reason-giving" (lines 25–27), but that does not mean mental processes are essentially a combination of those two activities.

(C) is a Distortion. Oxygen usage is mentioned in the third paragraph as part of the fMRI. Uttal makes no claim about oxygen, let alone that its usage is uniform throughout the brain.

(D) is a Faulty Use of Detail. The subtractive method is not mentioned until the third paragraph, and Uttal makes no claim about the method or what it can do.

26. (C) Inference

Step 2: Identify the Question Type

The correct answer will be "supported by the passage," making this an Inference question.

Step 3: Research the Relevant Text

With no line reference or content clues, the entire text is relevant.

Step 4: Make a Prediction

With no clues for reference, a specific prediction will be impossible. Stay focused on the big picture, and use content clues in the answer choices to do any necessary research.

Step 5: Evaluate the Answer Choices

(C) is supported by details in the third paragraph. Lines 34–37 directly state that the rate of oxygen use "stands as a measure of metabolic activity." Thus, the more activity there is, the more oxygen usage there is.

(A) is a 180. The author's point in the second paragraph is that mental activities in general do *not* depend on independent modules.

(B) is a Distortion. The results mentioned in the third paragraph merely suggest that the rate of oxygen usage in other areas is no higher than usual. That doesn't mean the rate is "close to zero."

(D) is Extreme. The baseline measurement is taken in a "control condition," one particular condition that occurs before completing a certain task. There is no suggestion what would be true in any region of the brain "at all times."

(E) is not supported. While the author would argue that several regions of the brain are functioning when one is angry, it's possible that only one region is functioning more than usual and thus would be the only one to "light up."

27. (B) Logic Reasoning (Parallel Reasoning)

Step 2: Identify the Question Type

The question asks for a situation that is "most analogous" to the interpretation described in the passage. That makes this a Parallel Reasoning question, such as those that are found in Logical Reasoning.

Step 3: Research the Relevant Text

The way fMRI scans are interpreted is described in the third paragraph.

Step 4: Make a Prediction

The fMRI scans are interpreted using the subtractive method. That involves starting with a control condition in which oxygen usage is measured throughout the brain. When a task is being performed, the original values are subtracted from the new values. Any region that is working more than normal is interpreted to be "associated solely with the cognitive task in question." The correct answer will describe another situation in which an area with greater-than-normal activity at one time is said to be the sole area associated with that activity.

Step 5: Evaluate the Answer Choices

(B) is correct. In this case, similar to how the brain is always active, shoppers are always coming to the store. However, the time when shopping increases is said to be the sole time people are affected by ads (just like when one area of the brain lights up due to greater-than-normal usage, it's assumed that that's the only part of the brain performing the task at hand).

(A) does not match, suggesting that one area was needed because it provided the most support. That's not the same as saying that area was *solely* responsible.

(C) does not match, suggesting that one area is affected the *most* because it uses more water than another area. However, that's not the same as saying that area is the *sole* area associated with an activity.

(D) does not match, comparing usage in two areas (home versus office) rather than making one area the sole one involved in a situation.

(E) does not match, comparing short-term to long-term effects. That has nothing to do with identifying an area solely responsible for a certain activity.

Section III: Logic Games
Game 1: Student Research Teams

Q#	Question Type	Correct	Difficulty
1	Acceptability	C	★
2	Must Be True	D	★★
3	Must Be False	D	★★
4	"If" / Could Be True	E	★
5	"If" / Must Be True	B	★★

Game 2: Mystery Novel Clues

Q#	Question Type	Correct	Difficulty
6	Acceptability	D	★
7	"If" / Could Be True	E	★
8	"If" / Could Be True	B	★★
9	"If" / Could Be True	D	★★
10	Could Be True	A	★★
11	Rule Substitution	B	★★

Game 3: Art Exhibition Paintings

Q#	Question Type	Correct	Difficulty
12	Partial Acceptability	A	★★
13	"If" / Must Be True	A	★★
14	"If" / Could Be True	E	★★
15	"If" / Must Be True	D	★★
16	"If" / Could Be True	B	★★
17	Could Be True	E	★★★
18	Must Be False (CANNOT Be True)	D	★★★

Game 4: Trading Buildings

Q#	Question Type	Correct	Difficulty
19	Acceptability	C	★★
20	Must Be False (CANNOT Be True)	A	★★★
21	"If" / Must Be True	A	★★★
22	"If" / Must Be True	E	★★★★
23	Must Be False (CANNOT Be True)	D	★★★

Game 1: Student Research Teams

Step 1: Overview

Situation: A teacher assigning students to two research teams

Entities: Five students (Juana, Kelly, Lateefah, Mei, Olga) and two teams (green and red)

Action: Distribution. Determine the team to which each student is assigned. There is also the added twist of determining who is the facilitator of each team. Some may classify this as a full-fledged Selection element, which would make the game a Hybrid. Either classification will result in a similar sketch.

Limitations: One team will have two members while the other team has three. Exactly one member on each team will be a facilitator.

Step 2: Sketch

List the students by initial and set up a table with two columns, one labeled "green" and the other "red." Each team will get at least two members, so add two slots to each column. One team will get the fifth slot. This is a rare instance in which it is possible to set up Limited Options without seeing a single rule. Number restrictions often provide important deductions, so set up two sketches. In the first sketch, the green team will get a third member. In the second sketch, the red team will get a third member.

Both sketches now contain all five slots to be filled. As for the facilitator, there are a couple of ways that could be indicated in the sketch. Either set aside the top slot in each column as the facilitator, and mark it with a "fac") or leave the slots alone and star or circle the student who gets selected as facilitator once it's determined.

Step 3: Rules

Rule 1 splits up Juana and Olga. One of them will be on the green team, and one of them will be on the red team. While the order is unknown, it's important to indicate that one slot will be taken up on each team. So, draw "J/O" in one slot on each team.

Rule 2 establishes Lateefah on the green team. Add an "L" to a slot on the green team.

Rule 3 establishes that Kelly is not a facilitator. Make a note of this to the side (e.g., K not fac).

Rule 4 establishes that Olga *is* a facilitator. Star O and/or make a note to the side (e.g., O = fac).

Step 4: Deductions

If they weren't set up ahead of time, Limited Options are worthwhile to consider based on the two numeric outcomes. Have two sketches. In one, Green gets three students and red gets two. In the other, green gets two students and red gets three.

In the first option, there are two spaces established on the green team: J/O in one and L in the other. On the red team, one space is established: O/J (whoever is not on the green team). That means M and K will be split up, one on the green team and one on the red team. Add "M/K" to the remaining slots on each team.

In the second option, the green team is filled up. The two spaces contain J/O and L. That means everyone else will fill up the red team: O/J (whoever is not on the green team), M, and K.

It is unknown who the facilitator is on either team in either option. Olga is definitely one of the two facilitators, but the Limited Options setup does not definitively place Olga. Expect questions to provide more information on that twist.

Step 5: Questions

1. (C) Acceptability

As with any Acceptability question, go through the rules one at a time, eliminating answers that violate those rules.

(A) violates Rule 1 by putting Juana and Olga on the same team. **(D)** violates Rule 2 by putting Lateefah on the red team. **(E)** violates Rule 3 by making Kelly a facilitator. **(B)** violates Rule 4 by not having Olga as a facilitator. That leaves **(C)** as the correct answer.

2. (D) Must Be True

The correct answer for this question must be true no matter what. Any answer that could be false will be eliminated.

Neither Juana nor Olga are assigned to either team with certainty. So, Juana could be on the green team, and Olga could be on the red team. That eliminates **(A)** and **(C)**. Lateefah could be a facilitator, but need not be. That eliminates **(B)**. Olga must be a facilitator (Rule 4), so only one other student could be a facilitator. Thus, it must be true that Juana and Mei are not *both* facilitators. Either one of them could be, but not both—otherwise, there would be three facilitators. Therefore, **(D)** must be true, and is thus the correct answer.

For the record, Kelly cannot be a facilitator (Rule 3), but Juana could be. That eliminates **(E)**.

3. (D) Must Be False

The correct answer to this question must be false no matter what. Any answer that could be (or even must be) true should be eliminated.

If the green team has three members, as it does in Option I, then Kelly could be assigned there along with Lateefah, and it's possible for Lateefah to be the facilitator. That eliminates **(A)**.

If the red team has three members, as it does in Option II, then Kelly and Mei could be assigned together. In that case, Mei could be the facilitator. That eliminates **(B)**.

Olga is a facilitator no matter what (Rule 4), and she could be on either team with Mei. That eliminates **(C)**.

Lateefah is on the green team (Rule 2) and could be a facilitator. In that case, Olga, who also has to be a facilitator (Rule 4) would have to be facilitator for the red team. With Olga on the red team, Juana would have to be on the green team (Rule 1). That means Juana and Lateefah would be on the same team. It's impossible for them to be on different teams if Lateefah is a facilitator. That makes **(D)** the correct answer.

For the record, Olga must be a facilitator (Rule 4). If Mei is also a facilitator, she would be the facilitator for a different team, as each team only has one facilitator. Thus, **(E)** is possible and can be eliminated.

4. (E) "If" / Could Be True

For this question, Lateefah is a facilitator, which could happen in either option. However, she must be the facilitator for the green team (Rule 2). That means Olga, who is also a facilitator (Rule 4), must be the one for the red team. That means everyone else (Juana, Kelly, and Mei) are not facilitators. With Olga on the red team, Juana will be on the green team. That leaves Kelly and Mei. At least one of them must occupy a space on the red team. It could be either one. The remaining student could take up a third spot on either team.

With that, only **(E)** is possible, making it the correct answer. The other answers all must be false because they place either Juana or Olga on the incorrect team.

5. (B) "If" / Must Be True

For this question, Mei is assigned to the green team, which can only happen in Option I (because in Option II, Mei is on the red team). The green team will also include Lateefah (Rule 2) and either Juana or Olga (Rule 1). That's three students on the green team. The red team will thus have the remaining two: Juana or Olga (whoever is not on the green team) and Kelly.

With Kelly on the red team, **(B)** is the correct answer. The remaining answers are all possible but need not be true.

Game 2: Mystery Novel Clues

Step 1: Overview

Situation: An author writing a mystery novel that has seven clues contained in seven chapters

Entities: Seven clues (R, S, T, U, W, X, Z)

Action: Strict Sequencing. Determine the order, by chapter, in which the clues appear.

Limitations: All clues are mentioned exactly once, with exactly one clue in each of the seven chapters. This is standard one-to-one sequencing.

Step 2: Sketch

Simply list the clues at the top, and set up a series of seven numbered slots to which the clues will be assigned.

R S T U W X Z

```
___ ___ ___ ___ ___ ___ ___
 1   2   3   4   5   6   7
```

Step 3: Rules

Rule 1 prevents T from being placed in chapter 1. Draw "~T" under the first slot.

Rule 2 creates a concrete Block of Entities. T is placed before W with exactly two spaces in between.

T ___ ___ W

Rule 3 dictates that S and Z cannot be placed consecutively, in either order.

S̶ Z̶
Z̶ S̶

Rule 4 dictates that W and X cannot be placed consecutively, in either order.

W̶ X̶
X̶ W̶

Rule 5 creates a block of U and X, which must be consecutive, in either order.

| U X | or | X U |

Step 4: Deductions

The Block of Entities with T and W is the most significant component of the game. There must be at least three spaces after T (two clues followed by W). That means T cannot be placed in chapters 5, 6, or 7. Moreover, T cannot be placed in chapter 1 (Rule 1). Thus, T can only be placed in chapters 2, 3, or 4. That means W can only be placed in 5, 6, or 7. These restrictions can be noted in several ways: Add "~T" under spaces 1, 5, 6, and 7, and add "~W" under spaces 1, 2, 3, and 4. Or, turn negatives into positives and draw "T" with three arrows pointing to spaces 2, 3, and 4 and "W" with three arrows pointing to 5, 6, and 7. Alternatively, you could draw out Limited Options, with T and W in 2, 5; or 3, 6; or 4, 7, respectively.

```
I)   ___ _T_ ___ ___ _W_ ___ ___
      1   2   3   4   5   6   7

II)  ___ ___ _T_ ___ ___ _W_ ___
      1   2   3   4   5   6   7

III) ___ ___ ___ _T_ ___ ___ _W_
      1   2   3   4   5   6   7
```

It's also helpful to note that W and X are duplicated in the rules. W is now limited to three spaces (5, 6, or 7). X cannot be next to W (Rule 4). While it may not be immediately apparent, some quick testing will show that X cannot be placed into chapter 6. If it were, then W would be in either 5 or 7, violating Rule 4. Thus, X cannot be placed into chapter 6. Furthermore, because X cannot be in chapter 6, U cannot be in chapter 7 because then it couldn't be placed next to X, violating Rule 5.

The deductions about X and U can be difficult to spot. Most of the game could be managed without those deductions (especially with a good number of "if" questions), but they are very useful for one question in particular. Also, be careful not to make improper deductions. For example, even though W is in one of the last three chapters, X could be there, too—as long as they're separated. So, X could be in chapter 7 as long as W is in chapter 5 (and vice versa). Similarly, even though X cannot be in chapter 6, U could still be in chapter 5—as long as X was in chapter 4. Remember that deductions should indicate what absolutely must or cannot happen, not what merely seems unlikely. Finally, R is never mentioned in any of the rules and is thus a Floater, which can be noted with an asterisk. It can potentially be in any chapter of the book. If done with Limited Options, the final Master Sketch may look like this, with a couple other minor deductions about where U can't be based on knowing X can't be in certain chapters:

```
           *
           R S T U W X Z

I)   ___ _T_ ___ ___ _W_ ___ ___     S̶Z̶
      1   2   3   4   5   6   7       Z̶S̶
                ~U  ~X      ~X  ~U

II)  ___ ___ _T_ ___ ___ _W_ ___     W̶X̶
      1   2   3   4   5   6   7       X̶W̶
                    ~U  ~X      ~X
                                ~U     ┌─────┐
                                       │ U X │
                                       │ or  │
III) ___ ___ ___ _T_ ___ ___ _W_      │ X U │
      1   2   3   4   5   6   7        └─────┘
                        ~U  ~X
```

Step 5: Questions

6. (D) Acceptability

As with any Acceptability question, go through the rules one at a time, and eliminate answers that violate those rules.

(B) violates Rule 1 by putting T in the first chapter. **(A)** violates Rule 2 by having *three* chapters separate T and W. No choice violates Rule 3. **(E)** violates Rule 4 by placing X and W in adjacent chapters. **(C)** violates Rule 5 by separating U and X. That leaves **(D)** as the correct answer.

7. (E) "If" / Could Be True

For this question, X is in chapter 1. That means U must be in chapter 2 (Rule 5). That leaves only two ways to separate T and W to satisfy Rule 2. T could be in chapter 3 with W in chapter 6, or T could be in chapter 4 with W in chapter 7. Use Options II and III from the Limited Options as a starting point, and then add in the additional information to test them more thoroughly.

In Option II, with T in 3 and W in 6, that leaves chapters 4, 5, and 7 for the remaining clues: R, S, and Z. S and Z cannot be consecutive (Rule 3), so one of them must be in chapter 7. The other one will be next to R in chapters 4 and 5.

$$\text{II)} \quad \underset{1}{X} \; \underset{2}{U} \; \underset{3}{T} \; \underset{4}{\_\_} \; \underset{5}{\_\_} \; \underset{6}{W} \; \underset{7}{S/Z}$$
$$\overset{R}{\underset{Z/S}{\diagdown\diagup}}$$

In Option III, with T in 4 and W in 7, that leaves chapters 3, 5, and 6 for the remaining clues: R, S, and Z. S and Z cannot be consecutive, so one of them must be in chapter 3. The other one will be next to R in chapters 5 and 6.

$$\text{III)} \quad \underset{1}{X} \; \underset{2}{U} \; \underset{3}{S/Z} \; \underset{4}{T} \; \underset{5}{\_\_} \; \underset{6}{\_\_} \; \underset{7}{W}$$
$$\overset{R}{\underset{Z/S}{\diagdown\diagup}}$$

With that, only **(E)** is possible and is thus the correct answer. Z could be the clue mentioned in chapter of 3 of Option III.

8. (B) "If" / Could Be True

For this question, U is in chapter 3. That means T must be in chapter 2 or 4—so, either Option I or Option III. X also must be next to U (Rule 5), so it also must be in chapter 2 or 4. The placement of T and U will also determine where W can go, so redraw both options. In Option I, T is in chapter 2, which places W in chapter 5. Because the question stem says U is in chapter 3, that means X must be in chapter 4 (Rule 5). However, that violates Rule 4 because W and X are consecutive. Thus, this option is impossible and can be eliminated.

$$\text{I)} \quad \underset{1}{\_\_} \; \underset{2}{T} \; \underset{3}{U} \; \underset{4}{X} \; \underset{5}{W} \; \underset{6}{\_\_} \; \underset{7}{\_\_}$$

In Option III, T is in chapter 4, which places W in chapter 7. X will be in chapter 2 in order to be next to U (Rule 4). That leaves chapters 1, 5, and 6 for the remaining clues (R, S, and Z). S and Z cannot be consecutive (Rule 3), so one of them must be in chapter 1. The other one will be next to R in chapters 5 and 6.

$$\text{III)} \quad \underset{1}{S/Z} \; \underset{2}{X} \; \underset{3}{U} \; \underset{4}{T} \; \underset{5}{\_\_} \; \underset{6}{\_\_} \; \underset{7}{W}$$
$$\overset{R}{\underset{Z/S}{\diagdown\diagup}}$$

Only **(B)** is possible, making it the correct answer.

9. (D) "If" / Could Be True

For this question, Z is in chapter 7. This means that Option III is out because W is in chapter 7 in that option. Only Options I and II are possible. Redraw out both options.

In Option I, T is in chapter 2 and W is in chapter 5. In that option, chapters 3 and 4 are the only consecutive chapters available for U and X to be adjacent (Rule 5). However, X cannot be next to W (Rule 4), so X will be in chapter 3 and U will be in chapter 4. That leaves S and R, but S cannot be next to Z (Rule 3). So, S is in chapter 1 and R is in chapter 6.

$$\text{I)} \quad \underset{1}{S} \; \underset{2}{T} \; \underset{3}{X} \; \underset{4}{U} \; \underset{5}{W} \; \underset{6}{R} \; \underset{7}{Z}$$

In Option II, T is in chapter 3 and W is in chapter 6. The block of U and X could go into either chapters 1 and 2 or chapters 4 and 5. Whichever chapters they occupy, R and S will fill in the remaining chapters. Any order and combination is possible with one exception: X cannot be in chapter 5 because it cannot be next to W (Rule 4).

$$\text{II)} \quad \underset{1}{\_\_} \; \underset{2}{\_\_} \; \underset{3}{T} \; \underset{4}{\_\_} \; \underset{5}{\underset{\sim X}{\_\_}} \; \underset{6}{W} \; \underset{7}{Z}$$
$$\boxed{UX/XU} \quad \boxed{RS/SR}$$

With that, only **(D)** is possible, making it the correct answer.

10. (A) Could Be True

The correct answer will be the only one that could be true. That means the remaining four answers are impossible.

R is a Floater and not directly restricted by any rules of the game. Thus, it seems perfectly likely that **(A)** could be true—that R could be in chapter 7. If this is correct, the remaining answers should be clearly false.

T cannot be in chapter 5 because there would not be enough room for two clues *and* W after it, violating Rule 2. That eliminates **(B)**. Similarly, W cannot be in chapter 3 because there would not be enough room for two clues *and* T before it, also violating Rule 2. That eliminates **(D)**.

If it were determined at the onset that X cannot be in chapter 6 and U cannot be in chapter 7, that would make it easy to eliminate **(C)** and **(E)**. Otherwise, some quick testing proves why those answers are impossible. If X were in chapter 6, then W could not be in chapters 5 or 7 (Rule 4). That would put W in chapter 4 at the latest. However, that would put T in chapter 1, which violates Rule 1—and W could not be earlier. So, X cannot be in chapter 6. That eliminates **(E)**. Consequently, U cannot be in chapter 7 because that would put X in chapter 6, which has already been determined as impossible. That eliminates **(C)**, confirming that **(A)** is the only answer possible and thus the correct answer.

11. (B) Rule Substitution

This question asks for a rule that could replace Rule 1 in the game and have the exact same effect. In other words, it must guarantee that T is not in chapter 1, but it also cannot add any new restrictions that weren't already in place.

A rule that eliminates U from chapter 2 is no help at all. Not only does it not prevent T from being in chapter 1, but it also restricts U in a way that wasn't originally true. U was allowed in chapter 2 from the beginning. That eliminates **(A)**.

If W is kept out of chapter 4, that would keep T out of chapter 1 based on Rule 2. This would reestablish the restriction of the original rule. And W couldn't be in chapter 4 from the original rules, so this adds no unwarranted restrictions. The effect is identical to the original Rule 1, making **(B)** the correct answer. For the record:

X being left out of chapter 6 was a deduction from the original rules. However, directly stating X is out of chapter 6 does not necessarily prevent T from being in chapter 1. The original rule is not established. That eliminates **(C)**.

If U is mentioned earlier than T, then T couldn't be first. That definitely reestablishes the original rule. However, U did not always have to be earlier than T, as seen in a sketch for the fourth question of the game. This adds an unwarranted restriction, eliminating **(D)**.

Having X before W was never required by the original rules, and this would not ensure that T is left out of the first chapter. Thus, this does not help reestablish the original rule. That eliminates **(E)**.

Game 3: Art Exhibition Paintings

Step 1: Overview

Situation: Student paintings being displayed at an art exhibition

Entities: Eight paintings, two for each student (Franz, Greene, Hidalgo, Isaacs) in one of two mediums (oil and watercolor), and four walls (1, 2, 3, 4) with two positions on each wall (upper and lower)

Action: Distribution. There are a lot of variables in this game, but the ultimate goal is to take the the eight paintings and determine the wall on which they hang and the position on that wall.

Limitations: Each student has two paintings for a total of eight paintings. Each wall has two positions for a total of eight positions. So essentially, there are eight paintings and eight spaces. For each student, one painting is an oil and one painting is a watercolor. So, there are four oils and four watercolors. Similarly, each wall has one upper and one lower position, so there are four upper positions and four lower positions. At this point, there is no limit to how many oils or watercolors appear on any given wall nor to how many oils or watercolors appear in any given position (upper or lower).

Step 2: Sketch

The fundamental basis here is to take eight paintings and assign them to the eight positions on the walls. So, start by listing the eight paintings. The eight paintings consist of two from each person, with each person having one oil and one watercolor. Each painting can be identified by an uppercase initial for the student paired with a lowercase letter to designate oil or watercolor: Fo, Fw, Go, Gw, Ho, Hw, Io, Iw.

Then, set up a table with four columns labeled 1–4. In each column, add two slots, one on top of the other. To the side, label the top slots "upper" and the bottom slots "lower."

$$F_o \; F_w \; G_o \; G_w \; H_o \; H_w \; I_o \; I_w$$

	1	2	3	4
upper	—	—	—	—
lower	—	—	—	—

Step 3: Rules

Rule 1 states that no wall can have two watercolors. That means each of the four watercolors must be on a different wall. Because there are only four walls, each wall will get one watercolor. The second painting on each wall would then have to be an oil. Essentially, this rule indicates that each wall will have one oil and one watercolor. However, it does not specify a position (upper or lower) for any wall. So, make a note to the side (e.g., each wall = 1 o and 1 w) or draw "o, w" under each column.

Rule 2 prevents any student from having both paintings on the same wall. This can be notated in several ways. You can draw each restriction individually (e.g., No FF) or you can use a variable to indicate the restriction algebraically (e.g., No XX). Or, you can simply make a shorthand note (Each wall = 2 diff. students).

Rule 3 prevents any wall from having paintings by both Franz and Isaacs.

Rule 4 establishes that one wall will have Greene's watercolor in the upper position and Franz's oil in the lower position. However, it could be any wall, so draw this to the side as a block.

Rule 5 establishes Isaacs's oil in the lower position of wall 4. Add "Io" to that slot, and cross it off the entity list.

Step 4: Deductions

There is a lot of information to work with here, so take some time to go through it thoroughly. It will save a ton of time with the questions.

Each wall has two paintings, one watercolor and one oil. One wall is already set: Gw in the upper position and Fo in the lower position. Another wall, wall 4, has Io in the lower position. The upper position has to be a watercolor. It cannot be Franz's (Rule 3), Greene's (Rule 4), or Isaacs's (Rule 2). Therefore, it must be Hidalgo's watercolor (Hw) in the upper position of wall 4.

	1	2	3	4
upper				H$_w$
lower				I$_o$

That leaves two more walls to be completed. There are four paintings left: Franz's and Isaacs's watercolors and Greene's and Hidalgo's oils. Franz's and Isaacs's watercolors cannot be together (Rule 3), so one wall will get Franz's watercolor and the final wall will get Isaacs's. Greene's and Hidalgo's oils will be split between those two walls, in either order. There is no way to determine which position any painting is in on either of these two walls.

In the end, all four walls are determined to some degree. One wall will have Gw on top and Fo on bottom. One will have Fw and either Go or Ho, in either order. One will have Iw and either Go or Ho (whichever one is not with Fw), in either order. The final wall is wall 4 with Hw on top and Io on bottom.

Step 5: Questions

12. (A) Partial Acceptability

In a Partial Acceptability question, start by going through the rules one at a time. Eliminate any answers that are clearly violated. If any answers remain, use any major deductions and consider the entities that are not listed.

Each answer only lists the paintings in the lower position of each wall. Without knowing what's in the upper position, it is impossible to test Rules 1–3 directly. However, **(D)** violates Rule 4 by having Greene's watercolor assigned to a lower position, and **(C)** violates Rule 5 by putting Isaacs's oil on wall 3, not wall 4.

The most efficient way to test the remaining answer choices is to consider any deduction that prevents a particular painting from being in a lower position. Wall 4 has Isaacs's oil in the lower position. So, the upper position has to be a watercolor. It cannot be Franz's (Rule 3), Greene's (Rule 4), or Isaacs's (Rule 2). Therefore, it must be Hidalgo's watercolor (Hw). Because Hidalgo's watercolor always has to be in an upper position, that eliminates **(B)** and **(E)**. That leaves **(A)** as the only acceptable answer.

13. (A) "If" / Must Be True

For this question, Isaacs's watercolor is displayed on wall 2 and Franz's oil is on wall 3. Franz's oil has to be in the lower position on wall 3 with Greene's watercolor in the upper position (Rule 4). Wall 4 is already complete with Isaacs's oil in the lower position and Hidalgo's watercolor in the top position. That leaves three paintings to be assigned: Franz's watercolor, Greene's oil, and Hidalgo's oil. Isaacs and Franz cannot have paintings on the same wall (Rule 3). So, with Isaac's watercolor on wall 2, Franz's watercolor must be on wall 1.

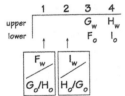

That makes **(A)** the correct answer. Greene's or Hidalgo's oil *could* be on wall 1, but only Franz's watercolor *must* be.

14. (E) "If" / Could Be True

For this question, Hidalgo's oil will be on wall 2. That means the other painting on wall 2 must be a watercolor (Rule 1 deduction). It cannot be Greene's watercolor (Rule 4), and it cannot be Hidalgo's watercolor (Rule 2). Thus, the other painting could only be either Franz's or Isaacs's watercolor, making **(E)** the correct answer. Likewise, looking back at the Deductions step, it was already determined that Hidalgo's oil

was in a Block of Entities with either Franz's watercolor or Isaacs's watercolor.

15. (D) "If" / Must Be True

For this question, Greene's oil is on the same wall as Franz's watercolor. It's already been established that one wall will have Greene's watercolor and Franz's oil (Rule 4), and wall 4 has Hidalgo's watercolor and Isaacs's oil. That means the remaining wall must have the two remaining paintings: Hidalgo's oil and Isaacs's watercolor.

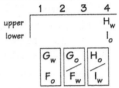

That makes **(D)** the correct answer. **(A)**, **(C)**, and **(E)** all make an upper/lower determination that could be, but does not have to, be, true. **(B)** is a violation of Rule 1.

16. (B) "If" / Could Be True

For this question, Franz's oil is displayed on wall 1. It must be in the lower position with Greene's watercolor in the upper position (Rule 4). Wall 4 is also established with Hidalgo's watercolor in the upper position and Isaacs's oil in the lower position. That leaves the remaining paintings, Franz's and Isaacs's watercolors and Greene's and Hidalgo's oils, for walls 2 and 3.

	1	2	3	4
upper	G_w			H_w
lower	F_o			I_o

With that, only **(B)** is possible, making it the correct answer.

For the record, **(A)** is a violation of Rule 3 given that Isaacs's oil is already established on wall 4 (Rule 5). **(C)** can be eliminated because Greene's watercolor must be on wall 1 along with Franz's oil (Rule 4). **(D)** can be eliminated because, as previously deduced in Step 4, Hidalgo's watercolor must be in the upper position on wall 4. Finally, **(E)** is a violation of Rule 5.

17. (E) Could Be True

The correct answer to this question will be the only one that could be true. The remaining answers must all be false.

Greene's watercolor must be in an upper position (Rule 4), so it's impossible for both of Greene's paintings to be in lower positions. That eliminates **(A)** and **(D)**.

Franz's oil must be in a lower position (Rule 4), so it's impossible for both of Franz's paintings to be in upper positions. That eliminates **(B)** and **(C)**. That leaves **(E)** as the correct answer.

One way this could look is this:

	1	2	3	4
upper	G_o	H_o	G_w	H_w
lower	F_w	I_w	F_o	I_o

18. (D) Must Be False (CANNOT Be True)

The correct answer to this question cannot be true, which means it will be false no matter what. That means the four wrong answers are all possible, if not definitely true.

The correct answer must be something definite. The definites given in the rules are Greene's watercolor in an upper position on the same wall as Franz's oil in a lower position (Rule 4), and Isaacs's oil in the lower position on wall 4 (Rule 5). With Isaacs's oil in the lower position, the upper position has to be a watercolor. It cannot be Franz's (Rule 3), Greene's (Rule 4), or Isaacs's (Rule 2). Therefore, it must be Hidalgo's watercolor (Hw). Because Hidalgo's watercolor always has to be in an upper position, **(D)** must be false and is thus the correct answer. All of the remaining answers are indeed possible.

Game 4: Trading Buildings

Step 1: Overview

Situation: Real estate companies looking to trade buildings

Entities: Three companies (RealProp, Southco, Trustcorp), eight buildings (Garza Tower, Yates House, Zimmer House, Flores Tower, Lynch Building, King Building, Meyer Building, Ortiz Building), and three building classes (1, 2, 3)

Action: Process. The buildings are already assigned classes, and they are already distributed among the three companies. The initial setup is provided in its entirety. The task is to take that initial setup and determine how things can be rearranged via a rule-driven process (in this case, the rules of trading). Process games are very rare on the LSAT and may be worth saving for last because they are often very unfamiliar.

Limitations: Because the initial setup is already complete, there are no limitations to find. The rules will provide all the limitations needed to answer the questions.

Step 2: Sketch

The sketch should illustrate the initial conditions of the game. In this case, there are three companies, each with a set of buildings. Set up three columns, one for each company. In each column, list the buildings each company owns by initial, along with a number to indicate its class (e.g., G1 for the class 1 Garza Tower in the RealProp column).

Real	South	Trust
G_1	F_1	K_2
Y_3	L_2	M_2
Z_3		O_2

Step 3: Rules

Rule 1 allows any company to transfer one building to another company in exchange for any one building of the same class (i.e., an even exchange).

Rule 2 allows any company to transfer one class 1 building to another company in exchange for two class 2 buildings.

Rule 3 allows any company to transfer one class 2 building to another company in exchange for two class 3 buildings.

Step 4: Deductions

The rules only provide information about what *could* happen. However, there is no indication of any trades that *must* happen. By the overview, the companies are merely *considering* trades. Thus, it is possible that one company decided not to trade anything at all. Of course, some trades are bound to happen—otherwise, this would be a very boring game.

The key here is to consider the implication of each rule to determine what could happen and what cannot happen. The first rule is the most useful. Companies are allowed to swap any two buildings of the same class at any time. That means that buildings of the same class are infinitely interchangeable. In other words, if a company has a class 2 building (e.g., Lynch Building), then that building can be exchanged for any other class 2 building at any time. This means it's ultimately more important to pay attention to the building classes than the building names. If you know a company has a class 2 building, it could effectively be any one of them. The same goes for class 1 and class 3 buildings.

The last two rules basically assign value to the building classes. Class 1 buildings are the most valuable and can only be obtained by trading two class 2 buildings. (This is like exchanging one $1 bill for two $0.50 coins.) Similarly, class 2 buildings are more valuable than class 3 buildings, again requiring two class 3 buildings to get a class 2 (i.e., like exchanging two $0.25 coins for a $0.50 coin).

$$\text{Class } 1 = \$1$$
$$2 = \$0.50$$
$$3 = \$0.25$$

There are only two class 1 buildings (Garza Tower and Flores Tower), but they require a lot to acquire. RealProp already has one, but only has two class 3 buildings in addition. Those class 3 buildings could be exchanged for a class 2 building, but that would not be enough to get the other class 1 building. Similarly, Southco has a class 1 building, but only has a single class 2 building in addition. Essentially, Southco has the same trading power as RealProp and thus cannot get both class 1 buildings, and Trustcorp starts with three class 2 buildings. Trustcorp can trade two of those buildings to get a class 1 building, but then it would have one class 1 building and just one class 2 building left. That's the same trading power as the other companies. Per the money exchanging analogy, each company has $1.50 worth of buildings. So, all companies have the same trading potential, with none of them able to get both class 1 buildings.

Finally, it helps to note that there are only two class 3 buildings, and they are both initially owned by RealProp. Because nobody else has a class 3 building, the only way to trade them is to exchange them *both* for a class 2 building. That would give another company both class 3 buildings. Once again, they could not be traded separately, so the two class 3 buildings will always be together—no matter who owns them.

Step 5: Questions

19. (C) Acceptability

The correct answer to this question will list a possible scenario after *only one* trade is made. That means only one rule will apply to the correct answer, but it's impossible to know which one. Unlike standard Acceptability questions, wrong answers here may not violate any rule—they may just apply too many. In this case, the answers have to be tested one at a time to make sure only one rule was applied.

In **(A)**, RealProp still has Garza Tower, but now has Flores Tower. However, that would require at least two trades because RealProp started with two class 3 buildings and those cannot be traded directly for a class 1 building. That eliminates **(A)**. Furthermore, as already deduced, no company can have both class 1 buildings ($2 of value).

In **(B)**, RealProp still has Garza Tower, but has traded its two class 3 buildings and somehow received two class 2 buildings. That violates the rules of trade and eliminates **(B)**.

In **(C)**, RealProp still has Garza Tower, but now has a class 2 building: Lynch Building. That could have happened by trading the two class 3 buildings (Yates House and Zimmer House) to the original owner of the Lynch Building: Southco. That is what's listed, and all of the buildings are where they started. That means only one acceptable trade was made, making **(C)** the correct answer. For the record:

In **(D)**, RealProp still has Garza Tower and the Yates House. However, RealProp now has Meyer Building (a class 2 building) in exchange for Zimmer House (a class 3 building). That's not an even exchange and is thus unacceptable. That eliminates **(D)**.

In **(E)**, RealProp has the same set of buildings it started with. Southco still has the Lynch Building, but now has the Ortiz Building (a class 2 building) in exchange for the Flores Tower (a class 1 building). That's not an even exchange and is thus unacceptable. That eliminates **(E)**.

20. (A) Must Be False (CANNOT Be True)

The correct answer to this question will be impossible, no matter how many trades are made. The four wrong answers will all be possible results.

RealProp starts with Garza Tower but only has two class 3 buildings to trade. Those could be traded for a single class 2 building, but that will still not be enough to ever trade for the Flores Tower, the remaining class 1 building. That means **(A)** can never happen and is thus the correct answer. For the record:

Southco starts with the Flores Tower. The other building it starts with is the Lynch Building, a class 2 building. That could be traded at any time for the Meyer Building, another class 2 building. That means **(B)** is possible.

Southco starts with the Lynch Building. The other building it starts with is the Flores Tower, a class 1 building. That could be traded at any time for the Garza Tower, another class 1 building. That means **(C)** is possible.

Trustcorp starts with the Ortiz Building. The other buildings it starts with are the King Building and the Meyer Building, both of which are class 2 buildings. Those could be traded together at any time for the Flores Tower, a class 1 building. That means **(D)** is possible.

Trustcorp starts with the Meyer building. The other buildings it starts with are the King Building and the Ortiz Building, both of which are class 2 buildings. Those two could be traded together at any time for the Garza Tower, a class 1 building. That means **(E)** is possible.

21. (A) "If" / Must Be True

For this question, RealProp will end up with only class 2 buildings. That means it must trade away its class 3 buildings and its class 1 building. Either remaining company can trade a class 2 building in exchange for the two class 3 buildings. However, neither remaining company could trade enough to get both class 1 buildings. Southco already has one but only has a class 2 building left to trade. TrustCorp has enough to trade for one class 1 building, but would be left with another class 2 building—not enough to get both. So, if RealProp has only class 2 buildings, then the two class 1 buildings must be split—one to Southco and one to Trustcorp.

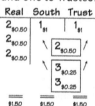

That means **(A)** must be true, making that the correct answer. For the record:

RealProp will have class 2 buildings, and all class 2 buildings are interchangeable. Thus, RealProp could end up with the Meyer Building, and not Trustcorp. That eliminates **(B)**.

Southco could trade its class 2 building for RealProp's class 3 buildings. That would leave Southcorp with a class 1 building and two class 3 buildings—no class 2 buildings. That eliminates **(C)**.

Alternatively, Southco could do nothing, and Trustcorp could trade for the class 3 buildings. That eliminates **(D)**.

Finally, Southco will end up with a class 1 building, as will Trustcorp. However, they could trade with each other, so either one could end up with the Flores Tower. That eliminates **(E)**.

22.(E) "If" / Must Be True

For this question, Trustcorp will end up with no class 2 buildings. Thus, it must trade all three class 2 buildings it starts with. It could trade two of those class 2 buildings for one of the class 1 buildings. That would leave it with one class 1 building and just one class 2 building. It wouldn't have enough to trade for *both* class 1 buildings, so it would have to trade the remaining class 2 building in exchange for the two class 3 buildings. That's the only way Trustcorp could end up without a single class 2 building.

```
Real   South   Trust
  |              1
  |               $1
  |              3
  |               $0.25
  |              3
  |               $0.25
```

So, Trustcorp would have a class 1 building and two class 3 buildings. The class 1 building could be either one (Flores Tower or Garza Tower), but there are only two class 3 buildings available. So, Trustcorp would have to end up with them both: Yates House and Zimmer House. Therefore, it must have the Zimmer House, making **(E)** the correct answer. For the record:

It's possible this happens with Trustcorp trading with RealProp the whole time, getting the Garza Tower for two class 2 buildings, and getting Yates House and Zimmer House for the remaining class 2 buildings. That would leave RealProp with no class 1 building, Southco with a class 1 building, and no trading done for Southco. That eliminates **(A)**, **(B)**, and **(C)**.

```
Real      South     Trust
 2          1          1
  $0.50      $1         $1
 2          2          3
  $0.50      $0.50      $0.25
 2                     3
  $0.50                 $0.25
 ===       ===        ===
 $1.50     $1.50      $1.50
```

Alternatively, that could all happen and Trustcorp could finally swap with Southco and take the Flores Tower in exchange for the Garza Tower. That eliminates **(D)**.

23.(D) Must Be False (CANNOT Be True)

The correct answer to this question cannot be true, which means it is impossible. The remaining answers will all be possible in some way.

RealProp could own three Class 2 buildings ($1.50 of value). Specifically, RealProp could trade its Garza Tower (class 1) with Trustcorp in exchange for the Meyer Building and the Ortiz Building (both class 2). Then, RealProp could trade its two class 3 buildings with Southco to get the Lynch building (class 2). That means **(A)** is possible and can be eliminated.

The Garza Tower is a class 1 building and the Meyer Building is a class 2 building—together a $1.50 value. Those are the same classes that Southco owns at the start, so Southco can certainly make even trades for those buildings. That eliminates **(B)**.

The King Building, the Meyer Building, and the Ortiz Building are all class 2 buildings owned by Trustcorp at the beginning ($1.50 of value). Southco could swap its class 2 building for any one of Trustcorp's and then trade its class 1 building for the other two. That means **(C)** is possible and can be eliminated.

The Yates House is a class 3 building. The only way for Trustcorp to get the Yates House is to trade a class 2 building for both Yates House *and* Zimmer House (the only other class 3 building). There's no way to have Yates House without Zimmer House, making **(D)** the correct answer.

For the record, Trustcorp could end up with the Garza Tower (class 1) and the Lynch Building (class 2)—together a $1.50 value. Specifically, Trustcorp could trade any of its class 2 buildings evenly with Southco to get the Lynch Building. Trustcorp could then trade its remaining class 2 buildings with RealProp to get the Garza Tower. That means **(E)** is possible and can be eliminated.

Section IV: Logical Reasoning

Q#	Question Type	Correct	Difficulty
1	Flaw	A	★
2	Point at Issue	C	★
3	Paradox	D	★
4	Strengthen	D	★
5	Assumption (Sufficient)	C	★
6	Principle (Identify/Inference)	A	★
7	Strengthen	B	★
8	Principle (Identify/Strengthen)	A	★★
9	Main Point	E	★
10	Strengthen	C	★★★★
11	Flaw	A	★
12	Inference	E	★
13	Paradox	A	★
14	Assumption (Sufficient)	E	★
15	Inference	E	★
16	Flaw	B	★
17	Inference	B	★
18	Assumption (Necessary)	E	★★★
19	Parallel Reasoning	B	★★
20	Assumption (Sufficient)	E	★★
21	Inference	B	★★
22	Strengthen/Weaken (Evaluate the Argument)	B	★★★★
23	Parallel Flaw	A	★★★
24	Principle (Apply/Inference)	E	★★★★
25	Weaken	D	★★★★
26	Flaw	B	★

1. (A) Flaw

Step 1: Identify the Question Type

The correct answer will describe why the given argument is "vulnerable to criticism," which is common wording for a Flaw question.

Step 2: Untangle the Stimulus

The organizer concludes that the community cleanup will be successful by having at least 100 participants. The evidence is that 85 residents have signed up and last year's cleanup had over 100 participants despite only 77 residents signing up.

Step 3: Make a Prediction

Based on last year's outcome, it's reasonable for the organizer to be optimistic. Unfortunately, one exceptional outcome is not enough to guarantee a similar outcome the next time. The correct answer will describe this use of one past experience to predict a future outcome.

Step 4: Evaluate the Answer Choices

(A) correctly describes the flaw. The community organizer certainly takes a single observation (what happened last year) and implies that it's a sign of a general trend that will repeat this year.

(B) is a Distortion. The organizer assumes that a similar *number* of people will participate, but not necessarily the same actual people.

(C) is not accurate. Nothing is ever described as required. The organizer merely claims the cleanup will be successful *if* there are 100 or more participants. That indicates sufficiency, not necessity.

(D) is not necessarily true. Only 77 residents signed up last year, but over 100 participated. Who are those extra people? They may very well be nonresidents, and the organizer does not ignore that possibility.

(E) is not accurate. No such term is defined, and the organizer merely predicts a positive outcome. The organizer never suggests that any outcome would be positive.

2. (C) Point at Issue

Step 1: Identify the Question Type

The stimulus consists of two speakers and the question asks for something about which those speakers disagree, making this a Point at Issue question.

Step 2: Untangle the Stimulus

Bell is defending Klein against critics, claiming that Klein is the kind of person we want making policy decisions. Klein's policies may have been unpopular, but they were effective. Soltan agrees that the policies worked, but suggests that the lack of support for Klein will prevent her from making important decisions in the future. Soltan thus suggests that Klein should step down.

Step 3: Make a Prediction

Bell and Soltan agree that Klein's policies have been effective. Unfortunately, they disagree about what that means going forward. Bell suggests that Klein should stick around, while Soltan argues she should leave office because of lack of support. The correct answer will bring up the dispute about Klein's future tenure in office.

Step 4: Evaluate the Answer Choices

(C) gets to the heart of the debate. Soltan makes this point directly, while Bell disagrees, suggesting we need Klein to stay.

(A) is a 180. Bell claims the policies were effective (they "avoided an impending catastrophe"), and Soltan *agrees* ("Klein's policies have been effective").

(B) is a 180. Bell likes the policies but admits that Klein has critics. Soltan agrees, claiming she doesn't have political support.

(D) is also a 180. Both Bell and Soltan directly state this very point.

(E) is not supported. Bell directly makes this claim. Soltan never suggests anything about an "impending catastrophe," but Soltan never disputes that claim, either.

3. (D) Paradox

Step 1: Identify the Question Type

The question asks for something that will "resolve the apparent discrepancy," making this a Paradox question.

Step 2: Untangle the Stimulus

The psychologist held a study that produced some mysterious results. Participants were asked how much they would pay for a particular mug. They said up to $5 and no more. They were then given a similar mug and asked how much they would sell it for; most of them wanted more than $5.

Step 3: Make a Prediction

Why would people put such a different price on a similar mug? It would appear they're following the philosophy of "a bird in the hand is worth two in the bush." In other words, they believe that something you have is worth more than something you don't.

Step 4: Evaluate the Answer Choices

(D) explains the difference in price. If people put a greater value on something they own, that explains why they would put a higher price on selling their own mug than on buying a similar mug they *don't* own.

(A) is a 180. The two mugs are similar. If people's assessment is based on the inherent properties of the mug, then the values should have been the same, not different.

(B) is Out of Scope. According to the psychologist, people who were given the mug were asked to value it "immediately afterwards." It doesn't matter how people act after possessing something for a long period of time.

(C) does not help. This might provide some insight into the price they devised in the first half of the experiment. However, it offers no explanation why they came up with a higher price when asked to sell their mug.

(E) is an Irrelevant Comparison, and likely a 180. They were only given mugs, so there's no need to draw a comparison between objects people were given and objects they bought. Besides, this suggests that people *undervalue* objects they were given. That just makes it more unusual that they gave a *higher* value to the mugs they were given.

4. (D) Strengthen

Step 1: Identify the Question Type

The question directly asks for something that will strengthen the given argument.

Step 2: Untangle the Stimulus

The ecologist starts by describing the nest-building behavior of male starlings. They decorate nests with plants that help kill parasites harmful to nestlings. Researchers thus argue that the decoration is used for that very reason: to protect nestlings. *However*, the ecologist argues otherwise, concluding that the decorations are actually meant to attract females. The evidence is that starlings stop adding such decoration once eggs are being laid.

Step 3: Make a Prediction.

The fact that decoration stops after eggs are being laid does seem to weaken the theory that the decorations are for nestling protection. However, the ecologist actually provides no evidence whatsoever that the decorations are used to attract females. The correct answer should make that much-needed connection.

Step 4: Evaluate the Answer Choices

(D) is correct, as it is the only answer that suggests a connection between the decorations and female starlings.

(A) is Out of Scope. This makes it clear that they don't need the greenery for their own protection, but it offers no support that the decorations are meant to attract females.

(B) is potentially a 180. This claims that starlings don't decorate their nests if they're in an area with few parasitic insects. That may be because the males have decided the aromatic plants are not necessary for protecting nestlings given that there's significantly fewer parasites around. This

strengthens the idea that the decoration is for protection against parasites, not for mating.

(C) is an Irrelevant Comparison. The speed at which nestlings grow offers no help to the ecologist's argument that the decorations are used to attract females.

(E) is Out of Scope. If this were true, it might explain why decoration would be used as protection for nestlings (which would actually strengthen the researchers' argument, not the ecologist's). However, it offers no support for the decoration being used to attract females.

5. (C) Assumption (Sufficient)

Step 1: Identify the Question Type

The question asks for something that, *if* assumed, would logically complete the argument. That makes this a Sufficient Assumption question.

Step 2: Untangle the Stimulus

The author concludes that the commission's report on disaster preparedness will not be effective. The evidence is that individual commission members have openly voiced their opinions, and effectiveness requires the commission to speak "with a unified voice."

Step 3: Make a Prediction

The key to this question is to pick up on the Formal Logic rule for effectiveness. The author claims that, for the report to be effective, the commission must speak in a unified voice.

If	effective	→	speak in unified voice

If the author believed the commission could *not* speak in a unified voice, that would be grounds to conclude the report will be ineffective.

If	~ speak in unified voice	→	~ effective

However, the author only claims that individual members have voiced their opinions ahead of time. So, the author is assuming that the voicing of opinions ahead of time will prevent the commission from speaking in a unified voice, thus making the report ineffective.

If	voicing opinions early	→	~ speak in unified voice	→	~ effective

Step 4: Evaluate the Answer Choices

(C) is correct. This makes it necessary for individual members to not speak out early. If they *did* speak out, this logic suggests that the commission couldn't speak in a uniform voice, as the author suggests. That would lead to the conclusion that the report will be ineffective.

If	speak in unified voice	→	~ voicing opinions early

(A) is Out of Scope. By the author's argument, the effectiveness of the report depends on the commission speaking in a unified voice, not the members' commitment to effectiveness.

(B) is Out of Scope. The author is not concerned about what should or should not happen, let alone making any judgment about the press. The author is merely trying to evaluate the effectiveness of the report.

(D) is also Out of Scope. This describes how the public might have reacted had the members *not* spoken out. However, the fact remains that the members *did* speak out, so this has no bearing on the author's argument about whether or not the report will be effective.

(E) is a Distortion. The conclusion's claim of ineffectiveness is based on commission members presenting opinions publicly before the report is complete. Whether or not they had opinions (which they may not have shared) before the commission was even *formed* plays no role in this argument.

6. (A) Principle (Identify/Inference)

Step 1: Identify the Question Type

The question asks directly for a principle that is used by the engineer. The correct answer will be a general rule that matches logically to the specific argument made by the engineer. That makes this an Identify the Principle question.

Step 2: Untangle the Stimulus

The engineer is arguing that blocking out some sun rays to cut back on global warming would actually have the opposite effect. People would just emit *more* carbon dioxide and make global warming worse. The evidence comes in the form of an analogy to driving. Making roads wider and obstacle-free actually makes things worse, as drivers are willing to take more risks.

Step 3: Make a Prediction

In both the engineer's argument about global warming and the supporting analogy about roads, the attempt to make things safer actually makes things worse because people then act more recklessly. The correct answer will express this general philosophy.

Step 4: Evaluate the Answer Choices

(A) matches the logic of both situations in the argument. In both cases, conditions are intended to appear safer (wider, obstacle-free roads and fewer sun rays causing global warming), but then people take more risks (driving more recklessly and emitting more carbon dioxide).

(B) is Extreme. This suggests that the "technical fix" for global warming is no good, so we have to bring in humans. However, the engineer never suggests that human-created solutions are *required*.

(C) is Extreme and a Distortion. The engineer just discusses how the solutions can make things worse. There is no mention of the solutions being "inevitably temporary."

(D) is Extreme. The solutions described *don't* discourage risk-taking behavior, but that doesn't mean other solutions *can't*. The engineer is just dismissing these solutions that try to provide a sense of security. There may be other, better solutions that do discourage risk-taking.

(E) is Out of Scope. The engineer makes no mention of how long global warming or narrow roads have been a problem. Likewise, nothing was mentioned about letting problems go unresolved.

7. (B) Strengthen

Step 1: Identify the Question Type

The question asks for something that "adds the most support" for the argument. That makes this a Strengthen question.

Step 2: Untangle the Stimulus

The author concludes ([*t*]*herefore*) that the oil urushiol did not evolve in plants for defense. The evidence is that urushiol, found in poison oak and poison ivy, causes a lot of pain for humans but hardly affects other animals, such as the wood rat.

Step 3: Make a Prediction

The author is suggesting that the painful rashes we experience are an anomaly. Urushiol is not supposed to be about protection, it just happens to be painful to us. To strengthen this, the correct answer will provide further evidence that our reaction is unique and/or urushiol normally does not provide much in the way of defense.

Step 4: Evaluate the Answer Choices

(B) strengthens the argument, providing further evidence that urushiol hardly offers plants a defense. Animals are *eating* the plant, despite the presence of urushiol.

(A) is Out of Scope, if not a 180. If wood rats wait until the plant is dead before using it, that could suggest that they avoid the plant while it's alive. In that case, it's possible the urushiol *does* provide defense.

(C) is a 180. This suggests that chemicals often *are* used as a defense, which does nothing to help the author's argument that urushiol is not.

(D) is Out of Scope. This just confirms how harmful urushiol could be to humans, but does nothing to support the author's argument about urushiol being non-defensive. If anything, it just makes urushiol sound worse and *more* likely to be a defense.

(E) is also Out of Scope. Where these plants grow does nothing to indicate the purpose of urushiol.

8. (A) Principle (Identify/Strengthen)

Step 1: Identify the Question Type

The correct answer will be a principle that will be used to *justify* a specific argument in the stimulus. That makes this an Identify the Principle question that acts like a Strengthen question.

Step 2: Untangle the Stimulus

The politician argues that we should not praise legislation that encourages renovation and revitalization in urban areas. The evidence is that such legislation only benefits wealthy professionals and winds up hurting the people it was supposed to help.

Step 3: Make a Prediction

The idea of renovation and revitalization sounds terrific, but the politician is disappointed in the ultimate effect: the people who were supposed to be helped are being displaced. In condemning the legislation, the politician is acting on the principle that legislation should not be praised if it doesn't help in the way it was intended.

Step 4: Evaluate the Answer Choices

(A) matches the politician's reasoning. The politician's evaluation of the legislation (it should not be commended) is based on the actual results (it displaced people who were supposed to be helped), despite the good intentions.

(B) is a Distortion. The politician is more concerned that wealthy people were benefiting from the legislation, not about any "undue influence" on their part to pass that legislation.

(C) is Extreme and a Distortion. The politician is concerned about the disparity in who's benefiting from legislation, not in how the legislation is being applied. Besides, the politician never goes so far as to say the legislation should apply *equally* to everyone.

(D) is Extreme. The legislation doesn't benefit *nobody*, it just didn't benefit who it was supposed to. The wealthy professionals still benefited.

(E) is a 180. The legislation in question did give well-to-do professionals an advantage, but it seems *not* to have benefited society as a whole because long-term residents were displaced. If there were unmentioned benefits to society as a whole, those would weaken the politician's argument that the legislation should not be commended.

9. (E) Main Point

Step 1: Identify the Question Type

The question asks for the "main conclusion" of the argument, making this a Main Point question.

Step 2: Untangle the Stimulus

The pundit starts off with a strong value judgment: it's good to vote leaders out of office after a few years. What follows is "[t]he reason," which indicates that the pundit is now providing evidence to support that first sentence. Reforms usually occur when new leaders first take over, and waiting too long to make reforms can lead to more problems.

Step 3: Make a Prediction

When there's a strong opinion followed by "[t]he reason" behind it, that's as good a sign as any that that opinion is the main point: it's good to have national leaders voted out after a few years.

Step 4: Evaluate the Answer Choices

(E) neatly sums up the first sentence, which is indeed the main point supported by everything else that follows.

(A) is not the conclusion. The pundit does imply this by stating that reforms are generally undertaken early in a new government. However, this is just evidence why the pundit concludes that national leaders *should* be voted out after a few years.

(B) is Extreme. Leaders can deny responsibility, but the last sentence suggests they can also admit responsibility. There is no indication of what tends to happen more often. Besides, this is all merely evidence anyway for why some leaders should be voted out.

(C) is not the conclusion. This is just evidence why it would be a good idea to vote out older leaders after a few years.

(D) is, if anything, a 180. The pundit never argues about letting leaders stay in office. The argument is about voting leaders *out* of office.

10. (C) Strengthen

Step 1: Identify the Question Type

The question directly asks for something that will strengthen the farmer's argument.

Step 2: Untangle the Stimulus

The farmer concludes ([*t*]*hus*) that agricultural techniques that don't use commercial products are generally only investigated by government-sponsored research. The evidence is that private companies won't sponsor such research without the potential for marketable (i.e., commercial) products.

Step 3: Make a Prediction

This is a common argumentative structure in which the author denies one option and concludes there is only one other solution. Such arguments ignore other solutions. In this case, when commercial products aren't involved, private corporations won't fund the research. So, the farmer concludes that only the government will. That assumes there are no other sources of funding for researching these agricultural techniques. The correct answer will strengthen this by denying any other options and/or making it more likely that only the government will get involved.

Step 4: Evaluate the Answer Choices

(C) strengthens the farmer's argument. This suggests, as the farmer assumes, that funding primarily comes from just two sources: private corporations and the government. So, if the private corporations are out, that just leaves the government.

(A) does not help. This suggests that the government will sponsor *some* research, but does not support the idea that it is the *only* source of sponsorship for such research.

(B) is Out of Scope. This suggests that noncommercial solutions are often viable, but does nothing to indicate who would sponsor research into those techniques.

(D) is Out of Scope. The argument is about who would sponsor noncommercial techniques. It doesn't matter who sponsors techniques that *do* use commercial products.

(E) is also Out of Scope. Even if the government focused primarily on sponsoring noncommercial techniques, it could still only be responsible for sponsoring research into just a small portion of those techniques. In that case, there would be plenty of other research that would have to be sponsored by someone else.

11. (A) Flaw

Step 1: Identify the Question Type

The correct answer will describe why the argument is "vulnerable to criticism." That's classic language indicating a Flaw question.

Step 2: Untangle the Stimulus

The spokesperson's conclusion comes at the very end: the university should rehire Hall Dining next year. The evidence is that the decision should reflect what most students want, and most students want a new food vendor. Hall Dining, for mysteriously unmentioned reasons, is the only viable option, despite the fact that Hall Dining was replaced last year by the current vendor.

Step 3: Make a Prediction

The ultimate goal of the spokesperson is to give the students what they want. However, the solution provided is to go back to the previous vendor. Perhaps there was a really good reason Hall Dining was dropped in the first place. Maybe students wanted them replaced last year and are just not happy with the current replacement. The spokesperson overlooks the possibility that going back to Hall Dining may not be the difference students were clamoring for.

Step 4: Evaluate the Answer Choices

(A) accurately describes a flaw in the reasoning. If the student didn't know that Hall Dining was the only other option, then there's a chance they won't be happy with the switch back. The spokesperson completely overlooks this possibility.

(B) mentions an unrepresentative sample, but there's no sample group to dispute.

(C) is Extreme. The spokesperson doesn't suggest that student preference is the *only* factor. It's just that it's important. Besides, the spokesperson *does* consider other factors—the mysterious "variety of reasons" that are referenced.

(D) is Out of Scope. The spokesperson does not discount some disagreement. The argument is merely based on satisfying the preference of "the majority of students."

(E) is a Distortion. Student preference is said to be important but not necessarily the *only* grounds on which this solution is based. Besides, there's no evidence that Hall Dining will be popular. In fact, the flaw is that the spokesperson overlooks the possibility it *won't* be popular.

12. (E) Inference

Step 1: Identify the Question Type

The correct answer will be "strongly supported by the information" given, making this an Inference question.

Step 2: Untangle the Stimulus

The author provides three comparisons between canned cat food and dry cat food: 1) cats fed canned cat food eat fewer ounces per day, 2) canned cat food has more calories per ounce, and 3) feeding a cat canned food costs more per day.

Step 3: Make a Prediction

There are a lot of possible inferences, so don't try to predict just one. Look for ways to combine the information provided to make deductions. It's important to note that none of the comparisons provide actual numbers. For example, cats that eat canned food eat fewer ounces, but how much is that? Does it eat a lot less or just a little? There's no way to tell.

That makes it difficult to make deductions with the second claim about calories. If cats that eat canned food tend to eat less, they could still take in fewer calories overall if the canned food was only slightly more caloric. However, if the canned food has many more calories, then cats could still take in more calories overall even with less food.

The last sentence, on the other hand, offers a deduction along with the first sentence. For cats that eat canned food, the daily cost is higher even though they're eating fewer ounces. That must mean their food must cost more per ounce.

Step 4: Evaluate the Answer Choices

(E) is supported. If it costs more per day to feed a cat canned food and cats eat fewer ounces per day, then canned cat food must be more expensive per ounce.

(A) is not supported. It's not known how big the difference in calories is. Cats that eat canned food eat fewer ounces per day. If the canned cat food has only a few calories more, then cats could still take in fewer calories overall by eating a lot fewer ounces than would a cat eating dry cat food.

(B) is not supported. The author only presents information about canned and dry food, but there could be other options that are just not mentioned and may be more common.

(C) is Extreme. While canned food is more expensive and has more calories, that doesn't mean calories are the *only* factor involved in the extra cost.

(D) is a Distortion. This only works if one assumes that "a cat that eats fewer ounces" refers to a cat that eats canned food, and "a cat that eats more ounces" refers to a cat that eats dry food. However, there may be a third food option that the author doesn't mention. It's possible that such an option *could* cost less with cats eating even fewer ounces per day than one eating canned or dry food.

13. (A) Paradox

Step 1: Identify the Question Type

The question asks for something that will "resolve the puzzle described," making this a Paradox question.

Step 2: Untangle the Stimulus

A foundation has reconstructed an historic church in Dresden so that it can be used for church services and other events. The foundation was determined to return the church to its original form. However, that leads to a puzzling exception: the organ. Instead of restoring the original baroque organ, the foundation built a new modern one.

Step 3: Make a Prediction

If returning the church to its original form is so important, why make an exception for the organ? Don't try to predict an exact solution. Just expect that the correct answer will describe why restoring the original organ was either infeasible or unacceptable.

Step 4: Evaluate the Answer Choices

(A) provides a solution. Restoring the original baroque organ would have to be inadequate for the church's current purposes.

(B) is Out of Scope. Even if modern organs have new features, this doesn't explain why those features would warrant the foundation going against its purpose to maintain the church's original form.

(C) is a 180. If the donation was intended solely for the purpose of restoring the original organ, it's even more unusual that the foundation ignored that request and went against the goal of bringing the church back to its original form.

(D) is Out of Scope. Even if the organ had been modified in the past, that doesn't mean it couldn't be restored to its original form. This offers no explanation why the foundation went in the other direction and made it more modern.

(E) is a 180. If the original organ was used for church services, then it's more unusual that the foundation didn't return it to its original form. It would have served the same purpose as it originally did.

14. (E) Assumption (Sufficient)

Step 1: Identify the Question Type

This is an unusual question stem, which can make it harder to identify. However, the stimulus contains a conclusion, and the correct answer will provide an unstated piece of information that, when added to the given evidence, will allow the conclusion to be properly drawn. That's the very essence of a Sufficient Assumption question.

Step 2: Untangle the Stimulus

The conclusion is that the government should not reduce import taxes on textiles. The evidence consists of two pieces of Formal Logic: 1) If reducing import taxes would benefit consumers, then it should be done. However, that could be superseded by 2) if reducing import taxes would significantly harm domestic industries, then it shouldn't be done.

Step 3: Make a Prediction

The first piece of Formal Logic provides a condition when the government *should* reduce taxes. However, the conclusion states that the government *shouldn't*, so that means the second overriding principle must be in effect. That states that taxes shouldn't be reduced if that would significantly hurt domestic industries. So, to reach the conclusion, the author is assuming that reducing taxes on textile imports would indeed cause significant harm to the industry. That would provide the grounds for rejecting the reduced taxes.

Step 4: Evaluate the Answer Choices

(E) provides the grounds for the conclusion. This suggests that reduced taxes would create significant harm, which is the very condition that would warrant saying *not* to reduce taxes.

(A) is a Distortion. While benefiting consumers would be grounds for reducing taxes, that doesn't necessarily mean that taxes should *not* be reduced without such a benefit. The only condition mentioned for not reducing taxes is if there's a significant harm.

(B) is a Distortion. The principle states that taxes should not be reduced if the industry will be "significantly harmed." Saying the textile industry won't benefit is not the same as saying it will be significantly harmed.

(C) is Out of Scope. Facing significant competition doesn't mean the industry is going to be harmed. It could thrive in the face of competition. This provides no grounds for stopping the reduction of taxes.

(D) is Out of Scope. Other measures don't affect the decision here. The only condition provided for denying the reduction of taxes is if the industry would be significantly harmed. Even if other measures provide a bigger benefit, it's still OK to lower taxes provided the industry is not harmed significantly. Thus, there would be no grounds for the conclusion to not reduce taxes on textile imports.

15. (E) Inference

Step 1: Identify the Question Type

The question asks for something that can "reasonably be concluded" from the information given. That conclusion will not be directly stated, but it will be an inference based on what's provided.

Step 2: Untangle the Stimulus

The author presents two ways in which global warming has led to rising sea levels: it causes glaciers and ice sheets to melt, and warmer water has more volume. *But* the author suggests the sea levels could have been even higher. That was prevented by artificial reservoirs, which hold water that would otherwise be in the sea.

Step 3: Make a Prediction

The author is essentially suggesting that there's more going on than people may realize. Sea levels may be rising, but that doesn't tell the whole story. Without the reservoirs, the levels would be even higher. There are a lot of potential conclusions to this situation. Don't predict one. Instead, test the answers and find one consistent with the facts without going too far or bringing in outside information.

Step 4: Evaluate the Answer Choices

(E) is supported. The rising sea level does give a glimpse into the effect of melting glaciers and ice sheets. However, some of that water may have also made its way into reservoirs, so the sea levels alone don't provide the complete picture.

(A) is not supported. The author does not suggest any dispute about how much the sea level has risen. The author merely suggests that there's more to consider than just the sea level.

(B) is not supported. The author provides no information about what occurred before reservoirs. If anything, it's likely that rising sea levels were caused by the same factors as now: melting ice and warmer water.

(C) is a 180. The author actually presents information about how global warming contributes to rising sea levels.

(D) is a Distortion. The author claims that global sea levels would have been higher without the reservoirs, but never says by how much. There is no foundation for this comparison.

16. (B) Flaw

Step 1: Identify the Question Type

The question directly asks for why the argument is *flawed*, making this a Flaw question.

Step 2: Untangle the Stimulus

The author concludes that Juan must have entered the software company's contest. The evidence is that Juan has a T-shirt with the company's new logo, and everyone who entered the contest got a T-shirt with that logo.

Evidence:

| *If* | *contest* | → | *T-shirt* |

Conclusion:

| *If* | *T-shirt* | → | *contest* |

Step 3: Make a Prediction

There could have been plenty of other ways for Juan to get a hold of that T-shirt. Maybe he works for the company. Maybe he bought one on the company's website. Maybe his friend entered the contest and gave him the shirt. Essentially, it boils down to a Formal Logic error. Entering the contest guaranteed people a shirt, but there's no indication that that was the only way to get a shirt (i.e., it wasn't necessary). The author reversed without negating.

Step 4: Evaluate the Answer Choices

(B) accurately describes this commonly tested flaw. Entering the contest was sufficient (i.e., it guaranteed getting a shirt), but the author acts as if it were necessary (i.e., Juan *must* have entered the contest to get that shirt).

(A) describes the commonly tested flaw of causation versus correlation, but the author is not concluding that one thing caused another to happen.

(C) is a Distortion. This describes another commonly tested flaw on the LSAT. However, the only group mentioned is people who entered the contest. The author does not draw an inference about *every* member of that group. The author only refers to Juan, who is not necessarily part of that group.

(D) describes circular reasoning, which means the evidence is based solely on the conclusion being true. However, the evidence is based on fact: Juan has the shirt. The conclusion need not be true for that evidence to be true.

(E) gets the logic backward. The author draws a conclusion about a single person (Juan) on the basis of a generalization (the general rule of contest entrants).

17. (B) Inference

Step 1: Identify the Question Type

For this question, the stimulus will "strongly support" the correct answer, meaning the correct answer will be a logical inference.

Step 2: Untangle the Stimulus

The author describes some problems with expert witnesses. Jurors often can't understand them and thus cannot evaluate their testimony. Even though expert witnesses can actually contradict one another, they can both appear competent. In that case, it's up to the jury to determine the reliability.

Step 3: Make a Prediction

This all leads to an unusual resolution. The final claim states that, when expert witnesses contradict one another, it's up to the jury to decide who is more reliable. However, the first sentence claims that juries often *can't*. In that case, juries are inevitably going to have to use a different basis for their decision.

Step 4: Evaluate the Answer Choices

(B) is exactly what the author is suggesting. If juries cannot understand and thus cannot evaluate expert testimony, they must base their decision on some other factor.

(A) is not supported. The author is not making any recommendations about what should or should not happen.

(C) is not supported. The information provided offers no suggestion about people who *can* understand the technical information, let alone their assessment of legal implications.

(D) is not supported. The author makes no recommendation about who should be selected for juries.

(E) is a 180. The author directly states that expert witnesses on opposite sides can make conflicting claims. There's no indication that they are likely to *agree* about anything.

18. (E) Assumption (Necessary)

Step 1: Identify the Question Type

The question directly asks for an assumption, and one on which the argument *depends*, making this a Necessary Assumption question.

Step 2: Untangle the Stimulus

The tax reformer concludes that the proposed tax legislation is perfectly framed. This is despite the fact that some people criticize the legislation for being too vague and some criticize it for being too specific. The reformer's evidence is that no one statement can be both too specific and too vague.

Step 3: Make a Prediction

The reformer makes one major slip. The evidence is that one *statement* cannot be too specific and too vague. However, the reformer's conclusion is about the entire legislation. The reformer overlooks the possibility that the complaints are about different statements. The reformer must assume everyone is complaining about the same statements, and thus they're just being whiny—the legislation is perfect as is.

Step 4: Evaluate the Answer Choices

(E) must be assumed. If the legislation *is* made up of a combination of vague and overly specific statements, then the criticisms may be valid. The reformer must assume otherwise to suggest the legislation is just right.

(A) is Out of Scope. Even if criticism on both sides is rare (which is hard to believe), that offers no connection to why the reformer believes the legislation is good as is.

(B) is Out of Scope. The reformer is not concerned about results. The entire argument is solely about the quality of the legislation itself.

(C) is also Out of Scope. It makes no difference to the reformer's argument whether these are the only two groups making criticisms or whether there are countless others.

(D) is Out of Scope, too. Who the legislation was meant to satisfy is immaterial. Using the Denial Test, even if the legislation *was* meant to satisfy one specific political group, and now the right and left have opposite complaints, that does not necessarily upend the tax reformer's conclusion that the legislation was framed "as it should be."

19. (B) Parallel Reasoning

Step 1: Identify the Question Type

The correct answer will be an argument "most similar" to the one presented in the stimulus. That makes this a Parallel Reasoning question.

Step 2: Untangle the Stimulus

The employee's company has blocked access to certain websites claiming they can be distracting. The employee counters that windows and decorations can also be a distraction, but those are not considered unacceptable.

Step 3: Make a Prediction

The employee is pointing out an inconsistency in the company's reasoning. The correct answer will do the same thing using similar logic: someone provides a reason why an action is unacceptable, but the author argues that the same reason does not make other actions unacceptable.

Step 4: Evaluate the Answer Choices

(B) matches the employee's call about inconsistency. Here, activists want to ban a device for the reason that extended exposure causes cancer in lab animals. However, the same reasoning does not make chemicals unacceptable.

(A) does not match. This just suggests everybody is different, and people fail to consider that sometimes. That's not the same as pointing out an inconsistency in applying the same reasoning.

(C) makes a prediction about a company needing to replace its retiring employees with new hires. This has nothing to do with suggesting that someone is applying reasoning in an inconsistent manner.

(D) does not provide inconsistent application of a reason. It merely claims that one thing (engaging characters) is not enough to guarantee a result (sales). That's not the same logic as the original.

(E) does not match. It rejects a standard of judgment because it's counterintuitive. Unlike the stimulus though, **(E)** does not indicate a discrepancy on how that standard is applied. The movie industry seems to always use that same standard.

20. (E) Assumption (Sufficient)

Step 1: Identify the Question Type

The question asks for something that, *if* assumed, would allow the conclusion to be drawn. That makes this a Sufficient Assumption question.

Step 2: Untangle the Stimulus

The author concludes ([t]*herefore*) that some students in French Lit 205 are not French-literature majors. The evidence is that some students in French Lit 205 are in Bio 218, and everyone in Bio 218 is a biology major.

Step 3: Make a Prediction

The evidence shows how some people in French Lit 205 are biology majors, but the author concludes that some people in that class are not French-literature majors. The author is simply assuming biology majors can't also be French-literature majors. If that were true, then the author's conclusion is confirmed. There are people in French Lit 205 who are not French-literature majors: the biology majors.

Step 4: Evaluate the Answer Choices

(E) is the assumption. If one cannot be both a biology major and a French-literature major, then those biology majors in French Lit 205 cannot be French-literature majors, confirming the author's conclusion.

(A) offers no support for the author's conclusion. If French Lit 205 is a requirement for French-literature majors, then there's no reason to suggest that anyone in that class is *not* a French-literature major.

(B) is Out of Scope. The author's argument is not about students in Bio 218. The argument is about students in French Lit 205.

(C) is an Irrelevant Comparison. It doesn't matter which major is more common at the university in general. The argument is only about who's taking the one class in question.

(D) is the same Irrelevant Comparison as **(C)** but reversed. It doesn't matter which major is more common at the university in general. The argument is only about who's taking the one class in question.

21. (B) Inference

Step 1: Identify the Question Type

The correct answer "must be true" based on the information given, making this an Inference question.

Step 2: Untangle the Stimulus

The stimulus consists of two pieces of Formal Logic: 1) in order for a book to be a literary classic, it must reveal something significant about people, and 2) if something is not worthy of serious study, then it doesn't reveal anything significant about people.

Step 3: Make a Prediction

As long as the Formal Logic is translated properly, the two statements can be combined. By the first statement, if a book is a classic, it must reveal something. Thus, by contrapositive, if it doesn't reveal anything, it can't be a classic:

If	*classic*	→	*reveal*
If	*~ reveal*	→	*~ classic*

By the second statement, if a book is not worthy of being studied seriously, it reveals nothing. By contrapositive, if it *did* reveal something, it *would* be worthy of serious study:

If	*~ worthy of serious study*	→	*~ reveal*
If	*reveal*	→	*worthy of serious study*

Putting these statements together, if a book is a literary classic, it must reveal something, which means it must be worthy of serious study. By contrapositive, if a book is not worthy of serious study, it reveals nothing, and thus cannot be a literary classic.

If	*literary classic*	→	*reveal*	→	*worthy of serious study*

If   ~ *worthy of serious study* →   ~ *reveal*   →   ~ *literary classic*

Anticipate that some, if not all, of the wrong answers will confuse sufficient and necessary conditions. Apply the logic properly, following the arrows in the right direction.

Step 4: Evaluate the Answer Choices

(B) directly follows the logic. In order for a book to be a classic, it must reveal something, which means it has to be worthy of serious study.

(A) is a classic trap, confusing necessary and sufficient conditions. Being worthy of serious study is necessary, but it does not guarantee that a book will be a classic.

(C) is a 180. Literary classics must reveal something about the human condition, which means they must be worthy of serious study.

(D) is possible, but does not have to be true. The logic only mentions what's true of books that are *not* worthy of serious study (they fail to reveal anything). There is no additional information guaranteed about books that *are* worthy of serious study.

(E) is possible, but does not have to be true. The logic only claims that literary classics reveal something about the human condition. There is no information guaranteed about books that are *not* literary classics. They might all reveal something as well. Don't dispute this as unlikely (which it very well may be). Instead, stay focused on the logic provided. The correct answer must be based on that and nothing else.

22. (B) Strengthen/Weaken (Evaluate the Argument)

Step 1: Identify the Question Type

The question asks for something that would "help in evaluating the argument." That makes this an Evaluate the Argument variant of Strengthen/Weaken questions. The correct answer will pose a question that, depending on how it's answered, would validate or invalidate the argument.

Step 2: Untangle the Stimulus

The author here is refuting an opinion. Scientists believed that the features of the *T. Rex* (large head, long legs, tiny arms) developed to accommodate the dinosaur's massive size. *However*, the author suggests abandoning this belief based on evidence of an earlier, much smaller dinosaur that had the same features.

Step 3: Make a Prediction

Paraphrased, the author's conclusion is that the *T. Rex*'s features did *not* develop to accommodate for the dinosaur's size. The evidence comes from another dinosaur skeleton with the same features at a fraction of the size of a *T. Rex*. This would definitely question the belief about accommodating a

larger animal . . . unless the skeleton found was of a baby dinosaur. It's highly unlikely that a *T. Rex* is *born* at full height. Perhaps the dinosaur in question was still quite young and would eventually grow to the same size as a *T. Rex*. In that case, the original hypothesis could still hold. For the author's argument to stand, it must be determined whether this new dinosaur skeleton was of a fully grown dinosaur or if it was just in its youth and yet to reach its full height.

Step 4: Evaluate the Answer Choices

(B) would help evaluate the author's argument. If the dinosaur was at the peak of its life, then the author has a point. If the dinosaur was still very young, it may have grown a lot more, and the feature could still serve to accommodate a larger animal.

(A) does not help. If the exact ratio was the same, that supports the author's claim for sure. However, even if the ratios were a little off, the general features were still the same and the author still has a point.

(C) is Out of Scope. The only comparison that's important here is between the *T. Rex* and the new dinosaur. How *T. Rex* compares to other dinosaurs has no effect on this argument.

(D) is Out of Scope. It doesn't matter if the dinosaurs were necessarily related. It's all about the size of the dinosaurs and the shared features.

(E) is also Out of Scope. It doesn't matter what size animals the dinosaurs preyed upon. All that matters are the features and why they developed.

23. (A) Parallel Flaw

Step 1: Identify the Question Type

The correct answer will be an argument with reasoning "most similar to" that in the given argument. That reasoning is said to be flawed, so this is a Parallel Flaw question.

Step 2: Untangle the Stimulus

The author concludes ([s]o) that the show *Bliss* must be the most watched show on television. The evidence is that *Bliss* is the most popular show on channel YXK, and YXK has more viewers than any other network.

Step 3: Make a Prediction

The problem is that what's true of a group comparison does not necessarily indicate what's true of individual members. In other words, just because the total viewers for YXK is the highest, that doesn't mean the same goes for each of its individual shows. It's possible that one other network has fewer viewers overall but has one outstanding show that is more popular than *Bliss*. The correct answer will commit the same error. It will claim that a group (YXK) has the highest number of something overall (most viewers), and then suggest that one member of that group (*Bliss*) has more than any other individual.

Step 4: Evaluate the Answer Choices

(A) matches the flawed logic. As with the original, this argument claims that a group (soccer players) has more of something (leg injuries) than any other group. The author then illogically claims that one member of that group (Linda) has more than any other individual. There may be one sport with fewer leg injuries overall, but which just happens to have one particular accident-prone player who got hurt more than Linda.

(B) is flawed, but not for the same reason. The evidence is about the number of awards received, while the conclusion makes a claim about being the *best* teacher. That's an unwarranted scope shift, but that's not what the original argument did wrong.

(C) is not flawed. This does not claim that the entire group (Olson Motor Company) sells the most cars. It states that the best-selling *individual* cars come from that company. So, it's logical to say its best-selling individual car is the best-selling individual car overall.

(D) is flawed, but not for the same reason. This uses extremes (highest- and lowest-paid individuals) to draw a conclusion about averages. This is not logical, but it's not the same flaw as the original, which had nothing to do with averages.

(E) does not match. This only focuses on what's true for an individual film. It does not try to apply what's true of an entire group to that individual. Furthermore, the level of certainty in **(E)**'s conclusion is *probably*. However the stimulus gave a more definitive conclusion.

24. (E) Principle (Apply/Inference)

Step 1: Identify the Question Type

The stimulus will contain a general principle that will be used to support the specific reasoning in the correct answer. That makes this an Apply the Principle question.

Step 2: Untangle the Stimulus

The stimulus provides two pieces of Formal Logic. First, for a contract to be valid, someone has to accept a legitimate offer. Second, if the person offered something reasonably believes the offer is in jest, then that offer is not legitimate.

Step 3: Make a Prediction

Once translated, the two statements can be combined. The first statement is that, if a contract is valid, there must be a legitimate offer. By contrapositive, if the offer is not legitimate, the contract is invalid.

	If	valid	→	offer legitimate
	If	offer ~ legitimate	→	~ valid

The second statement is that, if someone feels they are being offered something in jest, the offer is not legitimate. By contrapositive, for the offer to be legitimate, the person receiving the offer has to feel the offer is not in jest.

	If	offer believed to be in jest	→	offer ~ legitimate
	If	offer legitimate	→	offer ~ believed to be in jest

Combining these statements, for a contract to be valid, the offer must be legitimate, which means the person accepting the offer has to believe it was a serious offer. By contrapositive, it the person receiving the offer believes it's a joke, then the offer is not legitimate, and the whole contract is invalid. The correct answer will apply the Formal Logic properly without confusing necessary and sufficient conditions. Note that the correct answer doesn't have to use everything, it just has to be consistent.

Step 4: Evaluate the Answer Choices

(E) matches the logic of the principle. By the first statement, once the offer is illegitimate, the contract is invalid. This may have been difficult to choose as it doesn't apply the second half of the principle (regarding the offer being made in jest). However, it doesn't have to. As long as it doesn't contradict the second half (which it doesn't), it correctly applies the logic given, and is the only answer to do so.

(A) is a classic trap, as it gets the logic backward. To be valid, the offer *must* be legitimate. That means it's necessary. However, that does not mean it is sufficient, i.e., that every legitimate offer results in a valid contract. Furthermore, the fact that Sandy has not rejected the offer is not equivalent to accepting the offer.

(B) is a Distortion. If Kenta *believed* the offer was in jest, the contract would be invalid. However, Kenta didn't know that, and thus the principle provides no grounds to consider the contract invalid.

(C) is a Distortion. There is no condition that guarantees anyone accepting an offer. The *reasonable* standard of the stimulus was about whether or not an offer was legitimate, not whether or not it should be accepted.

(D) is a classic trap, as it gets the logic backward. Accepting a legitimate offer is necessary for a contract to be valid, but it is not sufficient, i.e., it does not guarantee the contract is certainly valid. Besides, the fact that nobody would believe the offer was in jest is also not sufficient to consider the offer legitimate. So this gets the logic of *both* statements backward.

25. (D) Weaken

Step 1: Identify the Question Type

The question directly asks for something that weakens the scientist's argument.

Step 2: Untangle the Stimulus

The scientist presents a timeline of events. Ages ago, there was a continent called Gondwana. That split up into the Americas and Australia. Long after that, a group of islands arose. On that island, there are certain species of iguana. Where did they come from? The scientist concludes they came from the Americas—all the way across the Pacific. They floated over on debris. The scientist doesn't think they came from Australia—even though the islands are surely closer to Australia—because the only existing species in the entire world related to the island iguanas are the ones in the Americas.

Step 3: Make a Prediction

The scientist makes a pretty good case, but makes one fatal error. The Americas is the only place in the world where a related species *currently* exists. The scientist overlooks the possibility that another related species once lived in Australia. Then, either they all migrated to the islands, or some of them migrated before the rest all died off in Australia. Either way, if related iguanas ever did live in Australia, the scientist's theory of iguanas travelling across an entire ocean on debris is suddenly called into question.

Step 4: Evaluate the Answer Choices

(D) weakens the scientist's argument. If there are fossils of related iguanas in Australia, then it's possible that the island iguanas migrated from there before the Australian population died off. There was no need for iguanas to travel across the ocean from the Americas.

(A) is Out of Scope. The argument is only about the iguanas, not any other animals on the islands.

(B) is Out of Scope. Even if there are *some* genetic differences, the two groups are still related, and the iguanas in the Americas are still the *only* related species in the world. So, **(B)** does not weaken the argument.

(C) does not weaken the argument either. Even if it's uncommon, that still means it could happen. In addition, the scientist has plenty of other evidence to make a case.

(E) is Out of Scope. The argument is only about the iguanas, and only about the ones that live on the islands. This answer talks about other immaterial plants and animals that live elsewhere.

26. (B) Flaw

Step 1: Identify the Question Type

The correct answer will describe why the argument is "vulnerable to criticism," which is wording that indicates a Flaw question.

Step 2: Untangle the Stimulus

Archaeologists recently found the largest tomb ever found in Macedonia. The author concludes that it must be the tomb of Alexander the Great. The evidence is that he was the greatest Macedonian in history and thus would have had the largest tomb.

Step 3: Make a Prediction

Sounds plausible, but what about the largest tomb that had been found before that? Did the author think *that* was Alexander the Great's? What if an even bigger tomb is found in the future? Maybe *that* will be the one that belonged to Alexander the Great—unless they find yet another one that's *even bigger*. All of this means the author is only basing a conclusion on what's been found so far without considering that other, bigger tombs have yet to be found.

Step 4: Evaluate the Answer Choices

(B) describes the author's mistake perfectly.

(A) is Extreme. The author suggests that Alexander's military success contributed to his greatness, but that doesn't mean that's the *only* way to attain greatness.

(C) is Out of Scope. The argument is only about Macedonia and Alexander as the greatest person in that area's history. It doesn't matter how the tomb compares to those in other regions.

(D) is Out of Scope. What happened after his death does nothing to change the status of all he accomplished when he was alive. The evidence still claims he was the greatest Macedonian in history. It was people *after* him that messed it all up.

(E) may be true, but it's not a logical flaw. It's perfectly reasonable to assume that the remains of a tomb can indicate the tomb's size. The flawed logic is assuming that archaeologists will never find anything bigger.

Glossary

Logical Reasoning
Logical Reasoning Question Types

Argument-Based Questions

Main Point Question

A question that asks for an argument's conclusion or an author's main point. Typical question stems:

> Which one the following most accurately expresses the conclusion of the argument as a whole?

> Which one of the following sentences best expresses the main point of the scientist's argument?

Role of a Statement Question

A question that asks how a specific sentence, statement, or idea functions within an argument. Typical question stems:

> Which one of the following most accurately describes the role played in the argument by the statement that automation within the steel industry allowed steel mills to produce more steel with fewer workers?

> The claim that governmental transparency is a nation's primary defense against public-sector corruption figures in the argument in which one of the following ways?

Point at Issue Question

A question that asks you to identify the specific claim, statement, or recommendation about which two speakers/authors disagree (or, rarely, about which they agree). Typical question stems:

> A point at issue between Tom and Jerry is

> The dialogue most strongly supports the claim that Marilyn and Billy disagree with each other about which one of the following?

Method of Argument Question

A question that asks you to describe an author's argumentative strategy. In other words, the correct answer describes *how* the author argues (not necessarily what the author says). Typical question stems:

> Which one of the following most accurately describes the technique of reasoning employed by the argument?

> Julian's argument proceeds by

> In the dialogue, Alexander responds to Abigail in which one of the following ways?

Parallel Reasoning Question

A question that asks you to identify the answer choice containing an argument that has the same logical structure and reaches the same type of conclusion as the argument in the stimulus does. Typical question stems:

> The pattern of reasoning in which one of the following arguments is most parallel to that in the argument above?

> The pattern of reasoning in which one of the following arguments is most similar to the pattern of reasoning in the argument above?

Assumption-Family Questions

Assumption Question

A question that asks you to identify one of the unstated premises in an author's argument. Assumption questions come in two varieties.

Necessary Assumption questions ask you to identify an unstated premise required for an argument's conclusion to follow logically from its evidence. Typical question stems:

> Which one of the following is an assumption on which the argument depends?

> Which one of the following is an assumption that the argument requires in order for its conclusion to be properly drawn?

Sufficient Assumption questions ask you to identify an unstated premise sufficient to establish the argument's conclusion on the basis of its evidence. Typical question stems:

> The conclusion follows logically if which one of the following is assumed?

> Which one of the following, if assumed, enables the conclusion above to be properly inferred?

Strengthen/Weaken Question

A question that asks you to identify a fact that, if true, would make the argument's conclusion more likely (Strengthen) or less likely (Weaken) to follow from its evidence. Typical question stems:

Strengthen

> Which one of the following, if true, most strengthens the argument above?

> Which one the following, if true, most strongly supports the claim above?

Weaken

> Which one of the following, if true, would most weaken the argument above?

> Which one of the following, if true, most calls into question the claim above?

Flaw Question

A question that asks you to describe the reasoning error that the author has made in an argument. Typical question stems:

The argument's reasoning is most vulnerable to criticism on the grounds that the argument

Which of the following identifies a reasoning error in the argument?

The reasoning in the correspondent's argument is questionable because the argument

Parallel Flaw Question

A question that asks you to identify the argument that contains the same error(s) in reasoning that the argument in the stimulus contains. Typical question stems:

The pattern of flawed reasoning exhibited by the argument above is most similar to that exhibited in which one of the following?

Which one of the following most closely parallels the questionable reasoning cited above?

Evaluate the Argument Question

A question that asks you to identify an issue or consideration relevant to the validity of an argument. Think of Evaluate questions as "Strengthen or Weaken" questions. The correct answer, if true, will strengthen the argument, and if false, will weaken the argument, or vice versa. Evaluate questions are very rare. Typical question stems:

Which one of the following would be most useful to know in order to evaluate the legitimacy of the professor's argument?

It would be most important to determine which one of the following in evaluating the argument?

Non-Argument Questions

Inference Question

A question that asks you to identify a statement that follows from the statements in the stimulus. It is very important to note the characteristics of the one correct and the four incorrect answers before evaluating the choices in Inference questions. Depending on the wording of the question stem, the correct answer to an Inference question may be the one that

- *must be true* if the statements in the stimulus are true

- is *most strongly supported* by the statements in the stimulus

- *must be false* if the statements in the stimulus are true

Typical question stems:

If all of the statements above are true, then which one of the following must also be true?

Which one of the following can be properly inferred from the information above?

If the statements above are true, then each of the following could be true EXCEPT:

Which one of the following is most strongly supported by the information above?

The statements above, if true, most support which one of the following?

The facts described above provide the strongest evidence against which one of the following?

Paradox Question

A question that asks you to identify a fact that, if true, most helps to explain, resolve, or reconcile an apparent contradiction. Typical question stems:

Which one of the following, if true, most helps to explain how both studies' findings could be accurate?

Which one the following, if true, most helps to resolve the apparent conflict in the spokesperson's statements?

Each one of the following, if true, would contribute to an explanation of the apparent discrepancy in the information above EXCEPT:

Principle Questions

Principle Question

A question that asks you to identify corresponding cases and principles. Some Principle questions provide a principle in the stimulus and call for the answer choice describing a case that corresponds to the principle. Others provide a specific case in the stimulus and call for the answer containing a principle to which that case corresponds.

On the LSAT, Principle questions almost always mirror the skills rewarded by other Logical Reasoning question types. After each of the following Principle question stems, we note the question type it resembles. Typical question stems:

Which one of the following principles, if valid, most helps to justify the reasoning above? (**Strengthen**)

Which one of the following most accurately expresses the principle underlying the reasoning above? (**Assumption**)

The situation described above most closely conforms to which of the following generalizations? (**Inference**)

Which one of the following situations conforms most closely to the principle described above? (**Inference**)

Which one of the following principles, if valid, most helps to reconcile the apparent conflict among the prosecutor's claims? (**Paradox**)

Parallel Principle Question

A question that asks you to identify a specific case that illustrates the same principle that is illustrated by the case described in the stimulus. Typical question stem:

Of the following, which one illustrates a principle that is most similar to the principle illustrated by the passage?

Untangling the Stimulus

Conclusion Types

The conclusions in arguments found in the Logical Reasoning section of the LSAT tend to fall into one of six categories:

1) Value Judgment (an evaluative statement; e.g., Action X is unethical, or Y's recital was poorly sung)

2) "If"/Then (a conditional prediction, recommendation, or assertion; e.g., If X is true, then so is Y, or If you an M, then you should do N)

3) Prediction (X *will* or *will not* happen in the future)

4) Comparison (X is taller/shorter/more common/less common, etc. than Y)

5) Assertion of Fact (X is true or X is false)

6) Recommendation (we *should* or *should not* do X)

One-Sentence Test

A tactic used to identify the author's conclusion in an argument. Consider which sentence in the argument is the one the author would keep if asked to get rid of everything except her main point.

Subsidiary Conclusion

A conclusion following from one piece of evidence and then used by the author to support his overall conclusion or main point. Consider the following argument:

> The pharmaceutical company's new experimental treatment did not succeed in clinical trials. As a result, the new treatment will not reach the market this year. Thus, the company will fall short of its revenue forecasts for the year.

Here, the sentence "As a result, the new treatment will not reach the market this year" is a subsidiary conclusion. It follows from the evidence that the new treatment failed in clinical trials, and it provides evidence for the overall conclusion that the company will not meet its revenue projections.

Keyword(s) in Logical Reasoning

A word or phrase that helps you untangle a question's stimulus by indicating the logical structure of the argument or the author's point. Here are three categories of Keywords to which LSAT experts pay special attention in Logical Reasoning:

Conclusion words; e.g., *therefore, thus, so, as a result, it follows that, consequently*, [evidence] *is evidence that* [conclusion]

Evidence word; e.g, *because, since, after all, for*, [evidence] *is evidence that* [conclusion]

Contrast words; e.g., *but, however, while, despite, in spite of, on the other hand* (These are especially useful in Paradox and Inference questions.)

Experts use Keywords even more extensively in Reading Comprehension. Learn the Keywords associated with the Reading Comprehension section, and apply them to Logical Reasoning when they are helpful.

Mismatched Concepts

One of two patterns to which authors' assumptions conform in LSAT arguments. Mismatched Concepts describes the assumption in arguments in which terms or concepts in the conclusion are different *in kind* from those in the evidence. The author assumes that there is a logical relationship between the different terms. For example:

> Bobby is a **championship swimmer**. Therefore, he **trains every day**.

Here, the words "trains every day" appear only in the conclusion, and the words "championship swimmer" appear only in the evidence. For the author to reach this conclusion from this evidence, he assumes that championship swimmers train every day.

Another example:

> Susan does **not eat her vegetables**. Thus, she will **not grow big and strong**.

In this argument, not growing big and strong is found only in the conclusion while not eating vegetables is found only in the evidence. For the author to reach this conclusion from this evidence, she must assume that eating one's vegetables is necessary for one to grow big and strong.

See also Overlooked Possibilities.

Overlooked Possibilities

One of two patterns to which authors' assumptions conform in LSAT arguments. Mismatched Concepts describes the assumption in arguments in which terms or concepts in the conclusion are different *in degree, scale, or level of certainty* from those in the evidence. The author assumes that there is no factor or explanation for the conclusion other than the one(s) offered in the evidence. For example:

> Samson does not have a ticket stub for this movie showing. Thus, Samson must have sneaked into the movie without paying.

The author assumes that there is no other explanation for Samson's lack of a ticket stub. The author overlooks several possibilities: e.g., Samson had a special pass for this showing of the movie; Samson dropped his ticket stub by accident or threw it away after entering the theater; someone else in Samson's party has all of the party members' ticket stubs in her pocket or handbag.

Another example:

> Jonah's marketing plan will save the company money. Therefore, the company should adopt Jonah's plan.

Here, the author makes a recommendation based on one advantage. The author assumes that the advantage is the company's only concern or that there are no disadvantages that could outweigh it, e.g., Jonah's plan might save money on marketing but not generate any new leads or customers; Jonah's plan might damage the company's image or reputation; Jonah's plan might include illegal false advertising. Whenever the author of an LSAT argument concludes with a recommendation or a prediction based on just a single fact in the evidence, that author is always overlooking many other possibilities.

See also Mismatched Concepts.

Causal Argument

An argument in which the author concludes or assumes that one thing causes another. The most common pattern on the LSAT is for the author to conclude that A causes B from evidence that A and B are correlated. For example:

> I notice that whenever the store has a poor sales month, employee tardiness is also higher that month. Therefore, it must be that employee tardiness causes the store to lose sales.

The author assumes that the correlation in the evidence indicates a causal relationship. These arguments are vulnerable to three types of overlooked possibilities:

1) There could be **another causal factor**. In the previous example, maybe the months in question are those in which the manager takes vacation, causing the store to lose sales and permitting employees to arrive late without fear of the boss's reprimands.

2) Causation could be **reversed**. Maybe in months when sales are down, employee morale suffers and tardiness increases as a result.

3) The correlation could be **coincidental**. Maybe the correlation between tardiness and the dip in sales is pure coincidence.

See also Flaw Types: Correlation versus Causation.

Another pattern in causal arguments (less frequent on the LSAT) involves the assumption that a particular causal mechanism is or is not involved in a causal relationship. For example:

> The airport has rerouted takeoffs and landings so that they will not create noise over the Sunnyside neighborhood. Thus, the recent drop in Sunnyside's property values cannot be explained by the neighborhood's proximity to the airport.

Here, the author assumes that the only way that the airport could be the cause of dropping property values is through noise pollution. The author overlooks any other possible mechanism (e.g., frequent traffic jams and congestion) through which proximity to the airport could be cause of Sunnyside's woes.

Principle

A broad, law-like rule, definition, or generalization that covers a variety of specific cases with defined attributes. To see how principles are treated on the LSAT, consider the following principle:

> It is immoral for a person for his own gain to mislead another person.

That principle would cover a specific case, such as a seller who lies about the quality of construction to get a higher price for his house. It would also correspond to the case of a teenager who, wishing to spend a night out on the town, tells his mom "I'm going over to Randy's house." He knows that his mom believes that he will be staying at Randy's house, when in fact, he and Randy will go out together.

That principle does not, however, cover cases in which someone lies solely for the purpose of making the other person feel better or in which one person inadvertently misleads the other through a mistake of fact.

Be careful not to apply your personal ethics or morals when analyzing the principles articulated on the test.

Flaw Types

Necessary versus Sufficient

This flaw occurs when a speaker or author concludes that one event is necessary for a second event from evidence that the first event is sufficient to bring about the second event, or vice versa. Example:

> If more than 25,000 users attempt to access the new app at the same time, the server will crash. Last night, at 11:15 pm, the server crashed, so it must be case that more than 25,000 users were attempting to use the new app at that time.

In making this argument, the author assumes that the only thing that will cause the server to crash is the usage level (i.e., high usage is *necessary* for the server to crash). The evidence, however, says that high usage is one thing that will cause the server to crash (i.e., that high usage is *sufficient* to crash the server).

Correlation versus Causation

This flaw occurs when a speaker or author draws a conclusion that one thing causes another from evidence that the two things are correlated. Example:

Over the past half century, global sugar consumption has tripled. That same time period has seen a surge in the rate of technological advancement worldwide. It follows that the increase in sugar consumption has caused the acceleration in technological advancement.

In any argument with this structure, the author is making three unwarranted assumptions. First, he assumes that there is no alternate cause, i.e., there is nothing else that has contributed to rapid technological advancement. Second, he assumes that the causation is not reversed, i.e., technological advancement has not contributed to the increase in sugar consumption, perhaps by making it easier to grow, refine, or transport sugar. And, third, he assumes that the two phenomena are not merely coincidental, i.e., that it is not just happenstance that global sugar consumption is up at the same time that the pace of technological advancement has accelerated.

Unrepresentative Sample

This flaw occurs when a speaker or author draws a conclusion about a group from evidence in which the sample cannot represent that group because the sample is too small or too selective, or is biased in some way. Example:

Moviegoers in our town prefer action films and romantic comedies over other film genres. Last Friday, we sent reporters to survey moviegoers at several theaters in town, and nearly 90 percent of those surveyed were going to watch either an action film or a romantic comedy.

The author assumes that the survey was representative of the town's moviegoers, but there are several reasons to question that assumption. First, we don't know how many people were actually surveyed. Even if the number of people surveyed was adequate, we don't know how many other types of movies were playing. Finally, the author doesn't limit her conclusion to moviegoers on Friday nights. If the survey had been conducted at Sunday matinees, maybe most moviegoers would have been heading out to see an animated family film or a historical drama. Who knows?

Scope Shift/Unwarranted Assumption

This flaw occurs when a speaker's or author's evidence has a scope or has terms different enough from the scope or terms in his conclusion that it is doubtful that the evidence can support the conclusion. Example:

A very small percentage of working adults in this country can correctly define collateralized debt obligation securities. Thus, sad to say, the majority of the nation's working adults cannot make prudent choices about how to invest their savings.

This speaker assumes that prudent investing requires the ability to accurately define a somewhat obscure financial term. But prudence is not the same thing as expertise, and the speaker does not offer any evidence that this knowledge of this particular term is related to wise investing.

Percent versus Number/Rate versus Number

This flaw occurs when a speaker or author draws a conclusion about real quantities from evidence about rates or percentages, or vice versa. Example:

At the end of last season, Camp SunnyDay laid off half of their senior counselors and a quarter of their junior counselors. Thus, Camp SunnyDay must have more senior counselors than junior counselors.

The problem, of course, is that we don't know how many senior and junior counselors were on staff before the layoffs. If there were a total of 4 senior counselors and 20 junior counselors, then the camp would have laid off only 2 senior counselors while dismissing 5 junior counselors.

Equivocation

This flaw occurs when a speaker or author uses the same word in two different and incompatible ways. Example:

Our opponent in the race has accused our candidate's staff members of behaving unprofessionally. But that's not fair. Our staff is made up entirely of volunteers, not paid campaign workers.

The speaker interprets the opponent's use of the word *professional* to mean "paid," but the opponent likely meant something more along the lines of "mature, competent, and businesslike."

Ad Hominem

This flaw occurs when a speaker or author concludes that another person's claim or argument is invalid because that other person has a personal flaw or shortcoming. One common pattern is for the speaker or author to claim the other person acts hypocritically or that the other person's claim is made from self-interest. Example:

Mrs. Smithers testified before the city council, stating that the speed limits on the residential streets near her home are dangerously high. But why should we give her claim any credence? The way she eats and exercises, she's not even looking out for her own health.

The author attempts to undermine Mrs. Smithers's testimony by attacking her character and habits. He doesn't offer any evidence that is relevant to her claim about speed limits.

Part versus Whole

This flaw occurs when a speaker or author concludes that a part or individual has a certain characteristic because the whole or the larger group has that characteristic, or vice versa. Example:

Patient: I should have no problems taking the three drugs prescribed to me by my doctors. I looked them up, and none of the three is listed as having any major side effects.

Here, the patient is assuming that what is true of each of the drugs individually will be true of them when taken together. The patient's flaw is overlooking possible interactions that could cause problems not present when the drugs are taken separately.

Circular Reasoning

This flaw occurs when a speaker or author tries to prove a conclusion with evidence that is logically equivalent to the conclusion. Example:

> All those who run for office are prevaricators. To see this, just consider politicians: they all prevaricate.

Perhaps the author has tried to disguise the circular reasoning in this argument by exchanging the words "those who run for office" in the conclusion for "politicians" in the evidence, but all this argument amounts to is "Politicians prevaricate; therefore, politicians prevaricate." On the LSAT, circular reasoning is very rarely the correct answer to a Flaw question, although it is regularly described in one of the wrong answers.

Question Strategies

Denial Test

A tactic for identifying the assumption *necessary* to an argument. When you negate an assumption necessary to an argument, the argument will fall apart. Negating an assumption that is not necessary to the argument will not invalidate the argument. Consider the following argument:

> Only high schools which produced a state champion athlete during the school year will be represented at the Governor's awards banquet. Therefore, McMurtry High School will be represented at the Governor's awards banquet.

Which one of the following is an assumption necessary to that argument?

(1) McMurtry High School produced more state champion athletes than any other high school during the school year.

(2) McMurtry High School produced at least one state champion athlete during the school year.

If you are at all confused about which of those two statements reflects the *necessary* assumption, negate them both.

(1) McMurtry High School **did not produce more** state champion athletes than any other high school during the school year.

That does not invalidate the argument. McMurtry could still be represented at the Governor's banquet.

(2) McMurtry High School **did not produce any** state champion athletes during the school year.

Here, negating the statement causes the argument to fall apart. Statement (2) is an assumption *necessary* to the argument.

Point at Issue "Decision Tree"

A tactic for evaluating the answer choices in Point at Issue questions. The correct answer is the only answer choice to which you can answer "Yes" to all three questions in the following diagram.

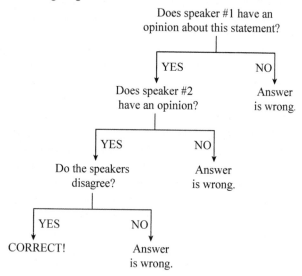

Common Methods of Argument

These methods of argument or argumentative strategies are common on the LSAT:

- Analogy, in which an author draws parallels between two unrelated (but purportedly similar) situations
- Example, in which an author cites a specific case or cases to justify a generalization
- Counterexample, in which an author seeks to discredit an opponent's argument by citing a specific case or cases that appear to invalidate the opponent's generalization
- Appeal to authority, in which an author cites an expert's claim or opinion as support for her conclusion
- Ad hominem attack, in which an author attacks her opponent's personal credibility rather than attacking the substance of her opponent's argument
- Elimination of alternatives, in which an author lists possibilities and discredits or rules out all but one

- Means/requirements, in which the author argues that something is needed to achieve a desired result

Wrong Answer Types in LR

Outside the Scope (Out of Scope; Beyond the Scope)

An answer choice containing a statement that is too broad, too narrow, or beyond the purview of the stimulus, making the statement in the choice irrelevant

180

An answer choice that directly contradicts what the correct answer must say (for example, a choice that strengthens the argument in a Weaken question)

Extreme

An answer choice containing language too emphatic to be supported by the stimulus; often (although not always) characterized by words such as *all*, *never*, *every*, *only*, or *most*

Distortion

An answer choice that mentions details from the stimulus but mangles or misstates what the author said about those details

Irrelevant Comparison

An answer choice that compares two items or attributes in a way not germane to the author's argument or statements

Half-Right/Half-Wrong

An answer choice that begins correctly, but then contradicts or distorts the passage in its second part; this wrong answer type is more common in Reading Comprehension than it is in Logical Reasoning

Faulty Use of Detail

An answer choice that accurately states something from the stimulus, but does so in a manner that answers the question incorrectly; this wrong answer type is more common in Reading Comprehension than it is in Logical Reasoning

Logic Games

Game Types

Strict Sequencing Game

A game that asks you to arrange entities into numbered positions or into a set schedule (usually hours or days). Strict Sequencing is, by far, the most common game type on the LSAT. In the typical Strict Sequencing game, there is a one-to-one matchup of entities and positions, e.g., seven entities to be placed in seven positions, one per position, or six entities to be placed over six consecutive days, one entity per day.

From time to time, the LSAT will offer Strict Sequencing with more entities than positions (e.g., seven entities to be arranged over five days, with some days to receive more than one entity) or more positions than entities (e.g., six entities to be scheduled over seven days, with at least one day to receive no entities).

Other, less common variations on Strict Sequencing include:

Double Sequencing, in which each entity is placed or scheduled two times (there have been rare occurrences of Triple or Quadruple Sequencing). Alternatively, a Double Sequencing game may involve two different sets of entities each sequenced once.

Circular Sequencing, in which entities are arranged around a table or in a circular arrangement (NOTE: When the positions in a Circular Sequencing game are numbered, the first and last positions are adjacent.)

Vertical Sequencing, in which the positions are numbered from top to bottom or from bottom to top (as in the floors of a building)

Loose Sequencing Game

A game that asks you to arrange or schedule entities in order but provides no numbering or naming of the positions. The rules in Loose Sequencing give only the relative positions (earlier or later, higher or lower) between two entities or among three entities. Loose Sequencing games almost always provide that there will be no ties between entities in the rank, order, or position they take.

Circular Sequencing Game

See Strict Sequencing Game.

Selection Game

A game that asks you to choose or include some entities from the initial list of entities and to reject or exclude others. Some Selection games provide overall limitations on the number of entities to be selected (e.g., "choose exactly four of seven students" or "choose at least two of six entrees") while others provide little or no restriction on the number selected ("choose at least one type of flower" or "select from among seven board members").

Distribution Game

A game that asks you to break up the initial list of entities into two, three, or (very rarely) four groups or teams. In the vast majority of Distribution games, each entity is assigned to one and only one group or team. A relatively common variation on Distribution games will provide a subdivided list of entities (e.g., eight students—four men and four women—will form three study groups) and will then require representatives from those subdivisions on each team (e.g., each study group will have at least one of the men on it).

Matching Game

A game that asks you to match one or more members of one set of entities to specific members of another set of entities, or that asks you to match attributes or objects to a set of entities. Unlike Distribution games, in which each entity is placed in exactly one group or team, Matching games usually permit you to assign the same attribute or object to more than one entity.

In some cases, there are overall limitations on the number of entities that can be matched (e.g., "In a school's wood shop, there are four workstations—numbered 1 through 4—and each workstation has at least one and at most three of the following tools—band saw, dremmel tool, electric sander, and power drill"). In almost all Matching games, further restrictions on the number of entities that can be matched to a particular person or place will be found in the rules (e.g., Workstation 4 will have more tools than Workstation 2 has).

Hybrid Game

A game that asks you to do two (or rarely, three) of the standard actions (Sequencing, Selection, Distribution, and Matching) to a set of entities.

The most common Hybrid is Sequencing-Matching. A typical Sequencing-Matching Hybrid game might ask you to schedule six speakers at a conference to six one-hour speaking slots (from 9 am to 2 pm), and then assign each speaker one of two subjects (economic development or trade policy).

Nearly as common as Sequencing-Matching is Distribution-Sequencing. A typical game of this type might ask you to divide six people in a talent competition into either a Dance category or a Singing category, and then rank the competitors in each category.

It is most common to see one Hybrid game in each Logic Games section, although there have been tests with two Hybrid games and tests with none. To determine the type of Hybrid you are faced with, identify the game's action in Step 1 of the Logic Games Method. For example, a game asking you to choose four of six runners, and then assign the four chosen runners to lanes numbered 1 through 4 on a track, would be a Selection-Sequencing Hybrid game.

Mapping Game

A game that provides you with a description of geographical locations and, typically, of the connections among them. Mapping games often ask you to determine the shortest possible routes between two locations or to account for the number of connections required to travel from one location to another. This game type is extremely rare, and as of February 2017, a Mapping game was last seen on PrepTest 40 administered in June 2003.

Process Game

A game that opens with an initial arrangement of entities (e.g., a starting sequence or grouping) and provides rules that describe the processes through which that arrangement can be altered. The questions typically ask you for acceptable arrangements or placements of particular entities after one, two, or three stages in the process. Occasionally, a Process game question might provide information about the arrangement after one, two, or three stages in the process and ask you what must have happened in the earlier stages. This game type is extremely rare, and as of November 2016, a Process game was last seen on PrepTest 16 administered in September 1995. However, there was a Process game on PrepTest 80, administered in December 2016, thus ending a 20-year hiatus.

Game Setups and Deductions

Floater

An entity that is not restricted by any rule or limitation in the game

Blocks of Entities

Two or more entities that are required by rule to be adjacent or separated by a set number of spaces (Sequencing games), to be placed together in the same group (Distribution games), to be matched to the same entity (Matching games), or to be selected or rejected together (Selection games)

Limited Options

Rules or restrictions that force all of a game's acceptable arrangements into two (or occasionally three) patterns

Established Entities

An entity required by rule to be placed in one space or assigned to one particular group throughout the entire game

Number Restrictions

Rules or limitations affecting the number of entities that may be placed into a group or space throughout the game

Duplications

Two or more rules that restrict a common entity. Usually, these rules can be combined to reach additional deductions. For example, if you know that B is placed earlier than A in a sequence and that C is placed earlier than B in that sequence, you can deduce that C is placed earlier than A in the sequence and that there is at least one space (the space occupied by B) between C and A.

Master Sketch

The final sketch derived from the game's setup, rules, and deductions. LSAT experts preserve the Master Sketch for reference as they work through the questions. The Master

Sketch does not include any conditions from New-"If" question stems.

Logic Games Question Types

Acceptability Question

A question in which the correct answer is an acceptable arrangement of all the entities relative to the spaces, groups, or selection criteria in the game. Answer these by using the rules to eliminate answer choices that violate the rules.

Partial Acceptability Question

A question in which the correct answer is an acceptable arrangement of some of the entities relative to some of the spaces, groups, or selection criteria in the game, and in which the arrangement of entities not included in the answer choices could be acceptable to the spaces, groups, or selection criteria not explicitly shown in the answer choices. Answer these the same way you would answer Acceptability questions, by using the rules to eliminate answer choices that explicitly or implicitly violate the rules.

Must Be True/False; Could Be True/False Question

A question in which the correct answer must be true, could be true, could be false, or must be false (depending on the question stem), and in which no additional rules or conditions are provided by the question stem

New-"If" Question

A question in which the stem provides an additional rule, condition, or restriction (applicable only to that question), and then asks what must/could be true/false as a result. LSAT experts typically handle New-"If" questions by copying the Master Sketch, adding the new restriction to the copy, and working out any additional deductions available as a result of the new restriction before evaluating the answer choices.

Rule Substitution Question

A question in which the correct answer is a rule that would have an impact identical to one of the game's original rules on the entities in the game

Rule Change Question

A question in which the stem alters one of the original rules in the game, and then asks what must/could be true/false as a result. LSAT experts typically handle Rule Change questions by reconstructing the game's sketch, but now accounting for the changed rule in place of the original. These questions are rare on recent tests.

Rule Suspension Question

A question in which the stem indicates that you should ignore one of the original rules in the game, and then asks what must/could be true/false as a result. LSAT experts typically handle Rule Suspension questions by reconstructing

the game's sketch, but now accounting for the absent rule. These questions are very rare.

Complete and Accurate List Question

A question in which the correct answer is a list of any and all entities that could acceptably appear in a particular space or group, or a list of any and all spaces or groups in which a particular entity could appear

Completely Determine Question

A question in which the correct answer is a condition that would result in exactly one acceptable arrangement for all of the entities in the game

Supply the "If" Question

A question in which the correct answer is a condition that would guarantee a particular result stipulated in the question stem

Minimum/Maximum Question

A question in which the correct answer is the number corresponding to the fewest or greatest number of entities that could be selected (Selection), placed into a particular group (Distribution), or matched to a particular entity (Matching). Often, Minimum/Maximum questions begin with New-"If" conditions.

Earliest/Latest Question

A question in which the correct answer is the earliest or latest position in which an entity may acceptably be placed. Often, Earliest/Latest questions begin with New-"If" conditions.

"How Many" Question

A question in which the correct answer is the exact number of entities that may acceptably be placed into a particular group or space. Often, "How Many" questions begin with New-"If" conditions.

Reading Comprehension
Strategic Reading

Roadmap

The test taker's markup of the passage text in Step 1 (Read the Passage Strategically) of the Reading Comprehension Method. To create helpful Roadmaps, LSAT experts circle or underline Keywords in the passage text and jot down brief, helpful notes or paragraph summaries in the margin of their test booklets.

Keyword(s) in Reading Comprehension

Words in the passage text that reveal the passage structure or the author's point of view and thus help test takers anticipate and research the questions that accompany the passage. LSAT experts pay attention to six categories of Keywords in Reading Comprehension:

Emphasis/Opinion—words that signal that the author finds a detail noteworthy or that the author has positive or negative opinion about a detail; any subjective or evaluative language on the author's part (e.g., *especially, crucial, unfortunately, disappointing, I suggest, it seems likely*)

Contrast—words indicating that the author finds two details or ideas incompatible or that the two details illustrate conflicting points (e.g., *but, yet, despite, on the other hand*)

Logic—words that indicate an argument, either the author's or someone else's (e.g., *thus, therefore, because, it follows that*)

Illustration—words indicating an example offered to clarify or support another point (e.g., *for example, this shows, to illustrate*)

Sequence/Chronology—words showing steps in a process or developments over time (e.g., *traditionally, in the past, today, first, second, finally, earlier, subsequent*)

Continuation—words indicating that a subsequent example or detail supports the same point or illustrates the same idea as the previous example (e.g., *moreover, in addition, also, further, along the same lines*)

Margin Notes

The brief notes or paragraph summaries that the test taker jots down next to the passage in the margin of the test booklet

Big Picture Summaries: Topic/Scope/Purpose/Main Idea

A test taker's mental summary of the passage as a whole made during Step 1 (Read the Passage Strategically) of the Reading Comprehension Method. LSAT experts account for four aspects of the passage in their big picture summaries:

Topic—the overall subject of the passage

Scope—the particular aspect of the Topic that the author focuses on

Purpose—the author's reason or motive for writing the passage (express this as a verb; e.g., *to refute, to outline, to evaluate, to critique*)

Main Idea—the author's conclusion or overall takeaway; if the passage does not contain an explicit conclusion or thesis, you can combine the author's Scope and Purpose to get a good sense of the Main Idea.

Passage Types

Kaplan categorizes Reading Comprehension passages in two ways, by subject matter and by passage structure.

Subject matter categories

In the majority of LSAT Reading Comprehension sections, there is one passage from each of the following subject matter categories:

Humanities—topics from art, music, literature, philosophy, etc.

Natural Science—topics from biology, astronomy, paleontology, physics, etc.

Social Science—topics from anthropology, history, sociology, psychology, etc.

Law—topics from constitutional law, international law, legal education, jurisprudence, etc.

Passage structure categories

The majority of LSAT Reading Comprehension passages correspond to one of the following descriptions. The first categories—Theory/Perspective and Event/Phenomenon—have been the most common on recent LSATs.

Theory/Perspective—The passage focuses on a thinker's theory or perspective on some aspect of the Topic; typically (though not always), the author disagrees and critiques the thinker's perspective and/or defends his own perspective.

Event/Phenomenon—The passage focuses on an event, a breakthrough development, or a problem that has recently arisen; when a solution to the problem is proposed, the author most often agrees with the solution (and that represents the passage's Main Idea).

Biography—The passage discusses something about a notable person; the aspect of the person's life emphasized by the author reflects the Scope of the passage.

Debate—The passage outlines two opposing positions (neither of which is the author's) on some aspect of the Topic; the author may side with one of the positions, may remain neutral, or may critique both. (This structure has been relatively rare on recent LSATs.)

Comparative Reading

A pair of passages (labeled Passage A and Passage B) that stand in place of the typical single passage exactly one time in each Reading Comprehension section administered since June 2007. The paired Comparative Reading passages share the same Topic, but may have different Scopes and Purposes. On most LSAT tests, a majority of the questions accompanying Comparative Reading passages require the test taker to compare or contrast ideas or details from both passages.

Question Strategies

Research Clues

A reference in a Reading Comprehension question stem to a word, phrase, or detail in the passage text, or to a particular line number or paragraph in the passage. LSAT experts recognize five kinds of research clues:

Line Reference—An LSAT expert researches around the referenced lines, looking for Keywords that indicate why the referenced details were included or how they were used by the author.

Paragraph Reference—An LSAT expert consults her passage Roadmap to see the paragraph's Scope and Purpose.

Quoted Text (often accompanied by a line reference)—An LSAT expert checks the context of the quoted term or phrase, asking what the author meant by it in the passage.

Proper Nouns—An LSAT expert checks the context of the person, place, or thing in the passage, asking whether the author made a positive, negative, or neutral evaluation of it and why the author included it in the passage.

Content Clues—These are terms, concepts, or ideas from the passage mentioned in the question stem but not as direct quotes and not accompanied by line references. An LSAT expert knows that content clues almost always refer to something that the author emphasized or about which the author expressed an opinion.

Reading Comp Question Types

Global Question

A question that asks for the Main Idea of the passage or for the author's primary Purpose in writing the passage. Typical question stems:

> Which one of the following most accurately expresses the main point of the passage?

> The primary purpose of the passage is to

Detail Question

A question that asks what the passage explicitly states about a detail. Typical question stems:

> According to the passage, some critics have criticized Gilliam's films on the grounds that

> The passage states that one role of a municipality's comptroller in budget decisions by the city council is to

> The author identifies which one of the following as a commonly held but false preconception?

> The passage contains sufficient information to answer which of the following questions?

Occasionally, the test will ask for a correct answer that contains a detail *not* stated in the passage:

> The author attributes each of the following positions to the Federalists EXCEPT:

Inference Question

A question that asks for a statement that follows from or is based on the passage but that is not necessarily stated explicitly in the passage. Some Inference questions contain research clues. The following are typical Inference question stems containing research clues:

> Based on the passage, the author would be most likely to agree with which one of the following statements about unified field theory?

> The passage suggests which one of the following about the behavior of migratory water fowl?

> Given the information in the passage, to which one of the following would radiocarbon dating techniques likely be applicable?

Other Inference questions lack research clues in the question stem. They may be evaluated using the test taker's Big Picture Summaries, or the answer choices may make it clear that the test taker should research a particular part of the passage text. The following are typical Inference question stems containing research clues:

> It can be inferred from the passage that the author would be most likely to agree that

> Which one of the following statements is most strongly supported by the passage?

Other Reading Comprehension question types categorized as Inference questions are Author's Attitude questions and Vocabulary-in-Context questions.

Logic Function Question

A question that asks why the author included a particular detail or reference in the passage or how the author used a particular detail or reference. Typical question stems:

> The author of the passage mentions declining inner-city populations in the paragraph most likely in order to

> The author's discussion of Rimbaud's travels in the Mediterranean (lines 23–28) functions primarily to

> Which one of the following best expresses the function of the third paragraph in the passage?

Logic Reasoning Question

A question that asks the test taker to apply Logical Reasoning skills in relation to a Reading Comprehension passage. Logic Reasoning questions often mirror Strengthen or Parallel Reasoning questions, and occasionally mirror Method of Argument or Principle questions. Typical question stems:

> Which one of the following, if true, would most strengthen the claim made by the author in the last sentence of the passage (lines 51–55)?

> Which one of the following pairs of proposals is most closely analogous to the pair of studies discussed in the passage?

Author's Attitude Question

A question that asks for the author's opinion or point of view on the subject discussed in the passage or on a detail mentioned in the passage. Since the correct answer may follow from the passage without being explicitly stated in it, some Author's Attitude questions are characterized as a subset of Inference questions. Typical question stems:

The author's attitude toward the use of DNA evidence in the appeals by convicted felons is most accurately described as

The author's stance regarding monetarist economic theories can most accurately be described as one of

Vocabulary-in-Context Question

A question that asks how the author uses a word or phrase within the context of the passage. The word or phrase in question is always one with multiple meanings. Since the correct answer follows from its use in the passage, Vocabulary-in-Context questions are characterized as a subset of Inference questions. Typical question stems:

Which one of the following is closest in meaning to the word "citation" as it used in the second paragraph of the passage (line 18)?

In context, the word "enlightenment" (line 24) refers to

Wrong Answer Types in RC

Outside the Scope (Out of Scope; Beyond the Scope)

An answer choice containing a statement that is too broad, too narrow, or beyond the purview of the passage

180

An answer choice that directly contradicts what the correct answer must say

Extreme

An answer choice containing language too emphatic (e.g., *all*, *never*, *every*, *none*) to be supported by the passage

Distortion

An answer choice that mentions details or ideas from the passage but mangles or misstates what the author said about those details or ideas

Faulty Use of Detail

An answer choice that accurately states something from the passage but in a manner that incorrectly answers the question

Half-Right/Half-Wrong

An answer choice in which one clause follows from the passage while another clause contradicts or deviates from the passage

Formal Logic Terms

Conditional Statement ("If"-Then Statement)

A statement containing a sufficient clause and a necessary clause. Conditional statements can be described in Formal Logic shorthand as:

If [sufficient clause] $\rightarrow$ [necessary clause]

In some explanations, the LSAT expert may refer to the sufficient clause as the statement's "trigger" and to the necessary clause as the statement's result.

For more on how to interpret, describe, and use conditional statements on the LSAT, please refer to "A Note About Formal Logic on the LSAT" in this book's introduction.

Contrapositive

The conditional statement logically equivalent to another conditional statement formed by reversing the order of and negating the terms in the original conditional statement. For example, reversing and negating the terms in this statement:

If $\quad A \qquad\qquad \rightarrow \qquad B$

results in its contrapositive:

If $\quad \sim B \qquad\qquad \rightarrow \qquad \sim A$

To form the contrapositive of conditional statements in which either the sufficient clause or the necessary clause has more than one term, you must also change the conjunction *and* to *or*, or vice versa. For example, reversing and negating the terms and changing *and* to *or* in this statement:

If $\quad M \qquad\qquad \rightarrow \qquad O\ AND\ P$

results in its contrapositive:

If $\quad \sim O\ OR \sim P \qquad\qquad \rightarrow \qquad \sim M$

CPSIA information can be obtained
at www.ICGtesting.com
Printed in the USA
LVOW02s0253020617

536600LV00021B/297/P

9 781506 223391